The Property Diaries

A story of buying a house,
finding a man & making a home
... all on a single income

Antonia Magee

Wrightbooks

First published in 2011 by Wrightbooks
an imprint of John Wiley & Sons Australia, Ltd
42 McDougall St, Milton Qld 4064

Office also in Melbourne

Typeset in ITC New Baskerville 11.3/14.3pt

© Antonia Magee 2011

The moral rights of the author have been asserted

National Library of Australia Cataloguing-in-Publication data:

Author:	Magee, Antonia.
Title:	The Property Diaries: A story of buying a house, finding a man and making a home ... all on a single income/ Antonia Magee.
ISBN:	9780730375845 (pbk.)
Subjects:	Housing Finance. House buying. Home ownership.
Dewey Number:	332.722

Cover design by Qualia Creative

Images: p. 86 © Christina Norwood/iStockphoto; p.100 © Anne Clark/iStockphoto

The table on p. 73 courtesy of <www.canstar.com.au>

Printed in Australia by Ligare Book Printer

10 9 8 7 6 5 4 3 2 1

Disclaimer

The material in this publication is of the nature of general comment only, and does not represent professional advice. It is not intended to provide specific guidance for particular circumstances and it should not be relied on as the basis for any decision to take action or not take action on any matter which it covers. Readers should obtain professional advice where appropriate, before making any such decision. To the maximum extent permitted by law, the author and publisher disclaim all responsibility and liability to any person, arising directly or indirectly from any person taking or not taking action based on the information in this publication.

This book is a work of fiction. Except as advised below, all people, companies and events in this work are fictional. Certain characters, while inspired by real people in the author's life, have been fictionalised for the purposes of this work. The individuals mentioned do not endorse the views, attitudes or opinions within this book, which are the author's alone.

Jason Cunningham, who is mentioned within this book, is not fictional, although certain comments and conversations made by him within the book may be fictionalised. Jason is a practising financial adviser, an author published by John Wiley & Sons Australia Ltd, and has been consulted in the development of this publication.

Contents

Acknowledgements

There are a few people who I would like to sincerely thank for helping *The Property Diaries* come together:

My editor Kelly, Mary from John Wiley & Sons, Dave and Dave from Qualia Creative, and Mortgage Choice.

My incredibly supportive family, especially Isobel, Madeleine, Max and George for letting me use their very cool names.

The three real estate gurus: Jason, Mal and Tim.

And to Steve, thank you for always being there.

Introduction

There comes a time in a woman's life when she has to make a decision: sit around waiting for 'The One' to come along so that things like houses, cars and life insurance can be taken care of by someone else; or bite the bullet, get her act together, and do it on her own. I, Maggie Rose, at the impressionable age of 32, bit the bullet and decided I wanted a house—without the husband and children to go with it.

Okay, so it's not revolutionary, but it is a reality. When I decided it was my time to get into the property game, it was on a whim after seeing a friend's fabulous apartment in New York City. My friend Grace seemingly had it all: the $3 million-plus home, the wealthy husband and a baby on the way. Although not quite in a position for marriage, the baby or the million-dollar digs, I knew I wanted the home.

In the year that followed, I learnt the hard way that there is no easy way to buy your first home. Because even if you have a generous set of parents, a huge salary or two incomes, buying a property takes a lot of hard work and patience. You have to be prepared to throw away your Saturdays to house-hunt, and you have to educate yourself on the rules and regulations of the real estate game.

One of the other sacrifices I had to make was leaving my lovely rental apartment, where I lived alone, to save some money. After my parents' faces turned a lighter shade of pale at the thought of their adult daughter moving back into the family home, I moved into a share house. I already had my finances on track, but it took me the entire year to save a deposit large enough that I could be confident putting my hand up at an auction... without thinking I was only playing make-believe.

If you're anything like me, it will take you a while to figure out what type of place you want to buy, save the deposit, get up the courage to have a credit check and finally apply for a loan. It's stressful but oh, so worth the effort. I made some pretty huge mistakes, but, thankfully, I had a great support network of people around me who had done it all before and helped me on the way to becoming a home owner.

Thrown into my real estate adventure was a mixed-up love life. I had always had an interesting track record with men, and in my year of searching for the key to the mortgage belt I also had to do a lot of soul searching about the men in my life. Thankfully, none of it stood in the way of me getting what I wanted: my own home.

So, after what felt like 1000 property inspections and 100 auctions, I found myself opening the door to my very own...

PART I

The swift kick

January to March

*Dream home: featured on the cover of Vogue
Living just last month*

Savings: $30750

Deposit needed: unknown

Happiness: anxiety setting in

'This *has* to be fate', I almost shouted to the extra-ordinarily handsome man sitting next to me. We were two hours into a flight to Australia from Los Angeles and I was too excited to sleep ... and just a bit tipsy.

'No, I mean it', I continued in an unusually shrill tone. 'I want to buy a house and you specialise in helping people get them!'

'Well, I'm not a real estate agent. I'm a lawyer and I draw up the contracts so the sales can proceed', Alex, the gorgeous lawyer, said to me over our third glass of champagne. 'I would, however, like to help *you* find a home, Maggie Rose', he added seductively as he pressed the button for a flight attendant to bring us another drink.

I had stopped at Los Angeles airport in transit on my way home from New York City. I'd immediately noticed the tall and dishevelled Alex in the airport lounge, but had not spoken to him. When I boarded the plane I'd been feeling miserable and had not been looking forward to the last, long leg of my flight home, but seeing him walk down the aisle towards me had instantly cheered me up. I was pleasantly surprised when he smiled and sat down beside me! He was immediately very chatty, and when the drinks trolley came around he ordered us both a glass of champagne and orange juice.

At first glance Alex looked more like a designer or an architect than a lawyer. He was wearing ripped jeans, an old, fitted shirt and a pair of very well-worn Converse sneakers. Very cute. He told me he specialised in property conveyancing. He had been in Chicago for business and, like me, was heading home to Australia via LA. Within an hour he had been telling me his dreams of legal grandeur and I told him all about my newfound desire to own my own home.

At the time I had felt that the stars had aligned by seating us next to each other. But anyone who has ever drunk more than three alcoholic drinks on a flight will be shaking their head at me right now. Because, unlike the champagne and orange juice Alex and I were drinking, alcohol and flying don't mix well. I don't know whether it was the low air pressure, the booze, or the combination of both, but what should have been a harmless mid-air flirtation turned into something much racier as, there in the emergency exit row, we proceeded to kiss passionately with our seatbelts on. Never a good look—I mean, we weren't even in first class.

Overseas flights are always longer than I remember them, but I must have lost some time on this one because the next thing I knew a hostess was gently tapping my shoulder to wake me up, and telling me to raise my seat forward to prepare to land. I didn't even have time to go to the toilet and clean myself up. My mouth was all furry, I had a thumping headache and all I could think about was drinking litres and litres of clean, fresh water.

In my state of extreme dehydration I hadn't immediately remembered kissing the passenger next to me, and it wasn't until Alex asked for my number that the horror of picking up on a plane came crashing back to me. Rather than engaging in any polite chitchat, I thought it best to just hand over a crumpled business card from the bottom of my handbag and pretend to fall back asleep until the flight landed.

Over the course of my life there have been several moments when I have wanted to be able to step out of my body and walk away in embarrassment, or just plain hit myself over the head with a cricket bat to stop myself from doing something stupid—that plane journey home was one of them. There I was, 32 years old and fresh from what had been a relaxing Christmas and New Year break in New York before the working year got off and running, thinking I was happy with my life. But upon leaving I got a swift kick in the guts that told me I needed to get my act together and sort out my life—and then I topped it off with the misjudgement of a drunken kiss.

I had enjoyed three amazing weeks in New York visiting my dear friend and fellow journalist Grace, but I had boarded the plane to leave feeling like a depressed basket-case. The depression had come over me as Grace and her husband, Sam, waved me off from the footpath outside their brand-new Upper West Side $3 million apartment. As I turned to wave to them from the back of the taxi, I could see Grace glowing, with her hand protectively over her 16-week-old baby bump, while Sam looked lovingly at his pregnant wife. Don't get me wrong, it had been a wonderful holiday, but seeing the smiling pair outside their fantastic building had left me feeling nothing but sick.

Grace had moved to New York two-and-a-half years earlier to work as a foreign correspondent for a news-paper. She was only supposed to stay for a year but had met Sam, a Wall Street stockbroker, and fallen in love. It was completely unlike her to fall in love with anyone appropriate. Within six months they were married and were living it up on his—from what I could gather from the calibre of their ritzy apartment—huge salary.

I had been expecting to join them on their late-night escapades in the cool restaurants and bars of Manhattan, but the night I arrived Grace had announced that she was 13 weeks pregnant, so there was to be no gallivanting around town; mostly just quiet dinners and then bed. Even New Year's Eve was spent at home, although I did manage to sneak out at 11.30 pm to meet up with a friend of a friend at a crazy bar called Mona's, where I danced until 5 am before stumbling back home to bed.

Now, it wasn't the husband or the baby that had upset me as I was leaving. Marriage and children were not on the agenda for me at that moment in time, and I was very happy for Grace. No—what had thrown me was the stunning apartment and the fact that the place was *theirs*. As the taxi drove through Manhattan towards the airport, I realised there was a real possibility that I would be renting my one-bedroom apartment for the rest of my adult life. And for some reason the idea of living on my own in someone else's home suddenly became the most depressing thought I'd had in years. A few drinks on the flight home hadn't made the feeling go away, either.

When the LA flight finally landed in Australia, I scrambled to get off the plane, leaving Alex in my wake.

I stood at customs feeling rotten. Alex was standing 10 metres away, smiling at me. I still had one more connecting flight to catch before arriving home, and Alex had told me he'd be on the same flight. I felt ill and embarrassed, and the thought of another hour in a plane feeling seedy, and possibly having to sit close to the man who just hours earlier I had been straining out of my seatbelt to get to, was too much to bear. I just wanted to get home as soon as possible. On my own.

To my relief I was given a reprieve from romantic liaisons for that last hour-long flight; I didn't even see where Alex was seated and he didn't try to find me. I sat alone at the back of the plane with a large bottle of water and tried to rehydrate.

I had arranged for Eliza, my best and oldest friend, to pick me up, and she was waiting at the gate with her one-year-old daughter when I arrived. I gave Eliza a hug and on her cue I turned around to see Alex waiting patiently.

'Alex, hi', Eliza said to him. I shot her a startled look. How did she know my in-flight fling? Could this be any more embarrassing?

'Hi, Eliza. I was just coming to say goodbye to Maggie. How do you two know each other?' Alex asked.

Eliza explained that I was her best friend and he told her we had been seated together on one of the flights. As we turned to leave, Alex leaned in and gave me a peck on the cheek, saying he would call me. I was mortified by my behaviour on the plane and could feel my cheeks blazing as we walked towards the car park. I couldn't help wondering what the flight stewards had been thinking as I disembarked that LA flight looking wildly dishevelled and thirsty.

As Eliza drove down the freeway towards my apartment she told me she had done her law degree with Alex.

I then gave her the rundown of my trip, the flight home and why I was feeling depressed.

'Lots of people get post-holiday blues, Maggie!' Eliza exclaimed.

'But this is different', I whined. 'I'm 32, single again and paying off someone else's mortgage so I can live alone. Grace has landed on her feet and seeing her in her beautiful new home just really hurt. It made me yearn for my own home but it feels so out of reach.'

'Don't be ridiculous', Eliza said. 'You are more than capable of having your own home without the rich husband. You have been saving like mad for three years and now you know what you want to do with it. You've even managed to meet a man on a plane; something most single women never even dream will happen to them.'

'I have no intention of seeing Alex again.'

'Why's that? He's lovely and very suave.'

'Suave?'

'Well, yeah. I don't think he has any trouble meeting women. And from the way he said goodbye to you just then, he clearly likes you. And you really need to get out and date people. You may be feeling depressed, but it's getting depressing being around you', Eliza said with a hint of annoyance.

'Thanks. You're a truly warm and good-hearted friend who feels she can say absolutely anything to me without any concern for my feelings', I bit back.

Eliza had recently returned to work at her legal practice three days a week, after a year of maternity leave. She was certainly back to her lawyerly ways. Unlike myself, who had only managed to financially get my act together as I hit 30, Eliza and her husband, Tom, owned two houses and were thinking about investing in a third.

Eliza had bought her first house alone at 29 and I knew I wasn't going to get any sympathy from her when it came to the pitfalls of being a responsible adult. So I changed the subject and told her about my trip for the rest of the drive home.

It was a Friday afternoon, and I only had the weekend to get over my jet lag before I had to return to my job as a journalist at *The City* newspaper on Monday, when real life would resume. After putting my bags down at the front door, jumping into a hot shower, and drinking what felt like five litres of water, I collapsed on my bed and slept for a solid 12 hours. The 5 am wake-up wasn't ideal and I wouldn't say I felt great but, compared to the horrendous hangover I'd had the evening before, I could have run a marathon.

In September two years earlier, I had received a promotion in the form of my very own column. The promotion had come after three years as a junior reporter slogging it out just to get a story in the paper, then one year of relative success as a crime reporter and a lifestyle blogger on *The City*'s website. The police beat had not exactly been my chosen career path but, coupled with the blog, I knew that if I kept my head down for a year or so something good was bound to come of the hard work. And it had. Unfortunately, though I had been doing my column for more than a year, several colleagues had made it clear that they did not think I was worthy of the position. And according to the former chief of staff and my former boss, Janice Green, I had gained my column through nothing short of favouritism. Nice.

I was by no means a big name at the paper, though. My job was to write a column twice a week, on whatever the editor wanted me to discuss, or on a topic I thought was worth following up. The column appeared on the bottom of the third, and the least important, opinion page. There was no photo next to my by-line, my name was never on the front page of the paper, and I was under no illusions that anyone, apart from my parents and friends, regularly read my stories. But having my own column had been a dream of mine since high school, and just before I had turned 31 it had become a reality. It was a chance to get my hands dirty and write about things I was interested in.

The days my column appeared in the paper it was also posted on *The City*'s website and I discussed the topics on a live blog the next day. The blog contributors were generally the same 30 or so people who liked to butt heads over whatever subject was on offer, but I liked many of them and, coupled with the column, the blog has been a big step up from the daily grind of crime reporting.

In November the previous year I had also picked up a regular spot on the talkback radio station Freedom AM, on top of my newspaper commitments. Once a week for 20 minutes I talked news with the host of Freedom's breakfast show. I was still relatively new to the radio spot and, again, I was not the star attraction; my editor had set up the gig for myself and four other *City* journalists. We all went on air one day a week each and were each paid the princely sum of just less than $100 for our efforts. Not bad money for 20 minutes' work. And the extra $5000 a year, as well as the extra money from my promotion at work, had boosted my annual income to $65 000.

All of this meant that I had to be on top of the news and, after three weeks without so much as turning on a computer, I was more than a little behind the latest stories.

I had decided to use the Saturday before my return to work to catch up on the most recent news events. But Grace's beautiful apartment kept popping into my head. I looked around my small, one-bedroom abode and realised I no longer wanted to be there. I got up from my desk and, walking from room to room, I found that whereas it had once looked light and airy, it had now started to look small and pokey.

My finances were a long way from where they had been three years earlier, when I had about $7000 in debts and couldn't pay my rent. Every cent of my $53 500 salary had been frittered away on dinners, clothes, hair appointments, too many nights out and anything else I could possibly spend money on. I had come a long way in the previous three years and I thought I deserved more than this tiny apartment. My salary had increased by more than $10 000 and I had the money in the bank to show for it.

I had been living on my own for 18 months and loved it. Moving out by myself had been the main prize after more than a year of scrimping to turn my battered finances around. After my major money crisis at the age of 29, I had spent a long year changing my ways. Gone were the frivolous spending and late nights out. And in their place was good old-fashioned budgeting that saw me save $10 000 in one year and clear my debts. No mean feat.

Two years later I had saved more than $30 000 and was pretty proud of myself. There had been fleeting plans to buy a house with my ex-boyfriend Spencer; however, those plans had fallen through when he accepted a job in Tokyo and we broke up. Since then, the closest I had been to owning a home was purchasing a subscription to *Vogue Living*. I had put home ownership out of my mind because I just didn't think I could do it alone.

I made myself a cup of tea before going back to my computer and trawling through the online newspapers and news websites to get myself up to date for work. It was obviously a slow news day; the top-ranked stories mainly covered the cricket—yawn—and my attention was quickly caught by the number of impressive-looking ads running down the side of the screen advertising 'Property riches', 'Competitive home loans' and 'Renovation salvation'. Before I realised what I was doing, I was clicking on the 'You wish' button in the property section of a news website and scrolling through the silver-tailed end of the real estate market.

I ogled over a house just a few streets away from my current apartment. It sounded *just* like me.

Property Description

THIS IS THE ONE YOU'VE BEEN WAITING FOR!

This beautiful single fronted Victorian terrace is simply stunning. With original period features and a spectacular modern rear renovation designed by renowned architecht Phillip Grip, this is a dream home for any couple.

The sleek open plan kitchen/dining area has Miele appliances. The large master bedroom overlooks the city and has an adjoining ensuite and an oak panelled walk-in wardrobe. A second large bedroom has access to the bright central bathroom. The north-facing courtyard is perfect for inner city living, as is the prime Leighton location. POA.

Contact
Adam Black
Discovery Real Esate
0476 999 999

email agent

Property Features and Amenities

Property type: house
Bedrooms: 2
Bathrooms: 2

view images

Leighton, where I currently lived, was a trendy inner-city suburb I adored. If I was ever going to buy a house, Leighton was where I wanted it to be. Filled with great cafés, restaurants and bars, to my mind it was the best suburb in the city. I had no idea what 'POA' meant—for all I knew it was referring to 'Pool Options Available', or maybe you needed 'Proof of Age' to buy it or there were 'Puppies on Arrival'.

However, with my interest piqued, I thought I'd just have a sneaky look at the other properties in the suburb and I found myself logging onto a real estate search engine that listed practically every property for sale on the local market. I didn't think a bank would ever consider me for a mortgage; my history with money was way too tainted. I just wanted to see what was out there.

The little I knew about buying real estate was that a house was a better investment than an apartment. That's what I'd heard other people say, anyway. I loved the idea of having my own home with a small garden, and not having to worry about (or hear!) neighbours above and below me. I could hear every move—and I mean every single move!—made by the couple who lived next door to me in my current building.

I put in a search request for two- or three-bedroom, two-bathroom houses for sale in Leighton. I had visions of a small Victorian house in one of Leighton's tree-lined streets going for around $400 000. I hadn't worried about entering in a price range—thinking most places would be pretty reasonable—and when the results page loaded I nearly choked.

The first house on the list said 'Renovators delight'. It was a three-bedroom house at the end of my street, which I walked past each day on my way to work. 'Renovators delight' was a *major* understatement; it needed a hell of a lot of work. The asking price was $700 000 to $750 000.

Surely the website had the price wrong. I may not have known a lot about the property market, but that seemed like a lot of money for a rundown house.

The next property said 'Perfect for first home buyers'. It was a two-bedroom, two-bathroom cottage on the edge of the suburb, with an asking price of $550 000. Still a lot of money, but it seemed to be in better condition than the decrepit house on my street. Then I clicked on the floor plan and realised why it was more reasonably priced. It really only had one bedroom plus a small study/ infant child's room, and one of the listed 'bathrooms' was a toilet majestically positioned at the far end of the backyard. Charming.

I kept searching and the cheapest house in Leighton I came across was a one-bedroom 1960s detached unit, overlooking a railway line and going for $450 000-plus. Not quite what I would have wanted if I ever dipped my foot into the property game. There were some stunning houses for sale though, and I fell in love with at least five in the two hours I was online. The really special places were going for at least $1 million and were way out of my league. Oh, and I had quickly worked out that 'POA' stood for 'Price on Application'…and what it really meant was 'Not Even In Your Dreams, Honey'!

With the idea of buying real estate put on the back-burner—and after a short nap!—it was time to really focus on work. To save myself from any more distractions, I walked down to my local café and grabbed the newspapers, deliberately leaving my mobile phone at home. It was one of the last times I would be alone and uncontactable for a while and I wanted to enjoy every second of it. I loved my job, but who likes going back to work after a holiday?

The City's front page had a story about an anonymous young Muslim woman who was begging for help to get out of an arranged marriage. My friend and colleague, Genevieve, had written the story. The other papers were covering the latest political scandal about a local politician who had been caught leaking confidential documents to the opposition. All interesting, and I started to get slightly excited about going back to work. I felt as though that old phrase 'A new year, a new beginning' had some credence after all.

When I returned to my apartment I checked my phone and saw that I had five missed calls and one text message. I was having dinner with my five closest friends at a local restaurant later that night and it seemed they had all decided to get in contact at once to remind me about it! The text message, however, wasn't from any of my friends; it was from Alex, the guy from the plane.

> 11:00 am
>
> Hi Maggie Rose. Lovely to meet you in transit. If you're around later this week I'd love to have another drink or two with you. Call me. Alex x

How did I get myself into these situations? I flinched at the hazy memory of the pair of us making complete fools of ourselves on the plane. I sat staring at the phone for a minute before deciding to wait until the next day to get back to him.

Two months before my trip to New York I had been set up with an architect called Julian by my old friend Max. Before then I hadn't been out with anyone since my ex, Spencer, had moved to Japan. The first three dates with Julian had been great fun—not mind-blowing or anything, just go-out-and-have-a-drink-and-idle-chitchat fun. But my heart just wasn't in it and the week before I went away I told him I wanted to be on my own for a while. He took it extremely well, which led me to think he hadn't been that keen on me, either. Anyway, as a consequence I thought it best to have a long hard think before accepting dates from anyone else for a while. No matter how handsome the person asking was.

Dinner was booked at Cucina, an Italian bistro that was about a five-minute walk from my place. On the way to the restaurant I decided to wander past the house I had seen for sale on my street. I wanted to see for myself how the owners could justify selling it for such a fortune. The facade of the house was in atrocious condition. It would have been a beautiful Victorian terrace in its day, but the screen door was hanging from its hinges and a window was smashed. Some of the bricks had even fallen from above the front door and were sitting smashed on the front porch.

The auction sign out the front said it was a deceased estate sale. Almost every night the previous summer, I had seen the old man that had lived there sitting on the porch. I hadn't seen him in months and it was only then that I knew why. It made the house seem even more downtrodden and forgotten than it already looked.

The house was on a corner, so I walked down the adjacent street and looked over the back fence. The garden wasn't much better than the front had been. The grass was a good half a metre high. The back of the house was a stock-standard brick wall that looked as if it would fall down with a big gust of wind, and I could see another wonky structure that I assumed was an outside laundry room.

Why on earth was this house on the market for more than $700 000? The man's family members were kidding themselves if they thought the house was worth any more than about $500 000 (in my opinion...as the expert I was!).

It was a hot summer's night and Eliza had booked a table for six outside the restaurant. Max and his wife, Jem, were already there when I arrived. Max was one of my oldest friends and I had become just as close to Jem when she and Max had started going out several years earlier.

'We heard you picked up on the plane', Max charmingly blurted out before I had even had a chance to sit down.

'Nice to see you, too. I had a great time with Grace in New York, thanks for asking', I replied sarcastically, trying to ignore what he'd said. Max always had something to say about my life and there was no knowing whether it was going to be good or bad. Despite our closeness, Max had an unbelievable capacity to rub me up the wrong way when he wanted to, even though I knew that his heart was always in the right place—it was his execution and timing that was often amiss. I quickly changed the subject onto how the renovations were going on their home.

Max's renovations were his new favourite subject. He was an architect and had designed the renovations on his house for Jem as sign of his love for her. Max could bang on about dodgy builders and plumbers for hours and for some reason he never got the hint when one of us tried to change the subject. While he yapped on, I started to think about the amount of work that would need to go into doing up the decrepit house for sale on my street.

'There's an awful house at the end of my street for sale and they are asking $700 000 for it. It's utter madness', I told them once Max had finished ranting.

'Yeah, I know the one', Max said. 'It's a massive block.'

'Still, that seems like a lot of money for a lot of work, doesn't it?'

'It's the land value, and that particular house also has loads of potential. The property market is going through the roof at the moment and Leighton is a very expensive suburb to buy into. Thinking about purchasing some real estate, Maggie?'

'It's crossed my mind.'

'Well, well, well, Maggie is going to take the plunge. Good for you! Let's just hope it's more straightforward than your initial attempts to save.'

He was a shocker. It was true, though—it had taken me six months to clear one measly credit card before I realised I needed to seek help for my hopeless inability to budget.

I was ever so thankful when Eliza and my good friends Fran and Tim arrived at that moment. Fran and Tim had previously been my housemates and, after a brief falling out over a late rent payment a few years earlier, we did our best to protect each other from Eliza and Max's domineering personalities and comfortable lifestyles.

I waited for them to sit down and order a drink before I told everyone about New York. I didn't want to let on to my mates (besides Eliza) that I had been left with a bittersweet taste in my mouth on leaving, so I glossed over the specifics. I told them how deliriously happy Grace was, that she was pregnant and that she possibly had the coolest apartment any of us would ever own.

Several of my close friends did actually own property by then. Eliza and her husband, Max and Jem, and now Grace and her husband owned their own houses, and Tim owned a restaurant (though not a house) with his partner, Yvette. Fran, however, was single and still living it up.

After dinner, Fran, Tim and I walked to a local bar to have a drink before heading home. They too had heard about my mid-air romance and I gave them a brief rundown. I didn't really want to talk about Alex; I needed to confess, to someone who would sympathise, that I was wildly jealous that Grace not only had a dream husband and a baby on the way but that she also owned an apartment. And now I wanted one, too.

'You should go for it', Tim cheered.

But Fran, rather than joining the talk about houses, looked at Tim and then at me, and said she had something important to tell me. Her tone immediately made me feel uneasy.

'I'm really, really sorry to have to be the one to tell you this, but I thought it was better coming from me than from someone at work', Fran said.

I had no idea what she might have been talking about. My immediate thoughts were that someone was dead, or I was going to lose my job and no-one had told me. Before I had gathered more thoughts, Fran said the two words I then realised I had been dreading hearing for a year.

'Spencer's back', she said.

Just hearing my ex-boyfriend's name made me feel as though I would be sick, or faint, or both.

'Are you sure?' I asked shakily.

'Sorry, Maggie, but yes. I saw him at the pub last week. He said he's back for good from Tokyo. And there's more bad news. He has a new girlfriend.'

My eyes had started stinging and I could feel tears forming.

'Well, thanks for letting me know', I answered, trying to control my quickening breathing. I didn't want to hear any more. I told Fran and Tim that jetlag had suddenly overwhelmed me and I needed to go home. Fran looked devastated and Tim just sat there in silence while I collected my bag and stood to go.

'I'll call you tomorrow, Maggie', Fran said.

'I'll be fine', I answered over my shoulder while walking out the door of the bar, hot tears now streaming down my cheeks.

The 10-minute walk home felt like an hour and, as soon as I was inside my apartment, I collapsed in a heap and started sobbing uncontrollably. Eventually dragging myself to my bedroom and undressing, I lay on the bed and took in what Fran had told me. 'Spencer is back', I said out loud to the air, which suddenly felt stifling. 'He is the last person I want to ever have to run into.'

Spencer and my incredible 18-month relationship (with one small hiccup a few months in) had ended in December just over 12 months earlier, when he accepted a job in Tokyo as the head of one of the leading television newsrooms in Asia. It was a messy break-up and we hadn't had any contact since a stilted conversation on the phone a few weeks after he had started his new job.

The Tokyo position had been a real coup for him and there was no way he was going to turn it down. I was devastated. He had asked me to go with him, but made it clear that he didn't know how long he would be away. He had also pointed out that I had just begun my columnist job at the paper. Eventually, after countless arguments and tears, he decided it was best if I didn't go with him. Spencer said he wanted us to stay together and do the long-distance thing, but I was angry, and told him it was over. Aside from him leaving, the fact that he didn't do cartwheels to try to convince me go with him broke my heart into a million tiny pieces.

I had felt betrayed. I genuinely thought he was 'The One' and in my mind that meant actually being together, not 10 000 kilometres apart. Was I just supposed to wait for him while he spent an indeterminate number of years living in Japan furthering his career? I didn't want to have to see him only when we had holidays—and neither of us would have been able to take an overseas holiday more than once every six months. I knew myself too well; the longing would have killed me. I was sure he'd known that, and that he hadn't been serious about us seeing each other long distance.

Spencer and I met at *The City*, where he was the star journalist and I was a relatively inexperienced 29-year-old reporter struggling along at the bottom of the career barrel. After a rocky start, I had fallen head over heels for him and just a month before he was offered the job we had started talking about buying a house together—a conversation I thought was heading in the direction of a marriage proposal. We were best friends and I had wanted to spend my life with no-one other than him.

And now he was back in town and had a new girl-friend. It didn't seem right that he had moved on so quickly. I know I had briefly seen someone before New York, but at the bottom of my heart I never thought Spencer would ever give up on us. Clearly I was delusional.

I rolled over and continued to cry into the pillow, hoping he wasn't coming back to work at *The City*. When I finally stopped crying, I got angry. 'If he's moved on, then I'm going to as well!' I said aloud. It was as though I was going through a fast-forward version of the seven stages of grieving, but in 10 minutes rather than 10 months!

I rolled over and grabbed my phone out of my bag. I sent Alex the lawyer a text message accepting his offer of a date.

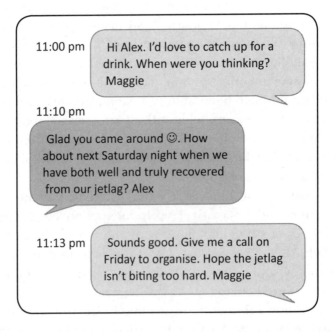

11:00 pm — Hi Alex. I'd love to catch up for a drink. When were you thinking? Maggie

11:10 pm — Glad you came around ☺. How about next Saturday night when we have both well and truly recovered from our jetlag? Alex

11:13 pm — Sounds good. Give me a call on Friday to organise. Hope the jetlag isn't biting too hard. Maggie

Monday morning came around and I was still exhausted, and still a little upset about Spencer being back. The lift doors opened to let me out into the office and I made a beeline for my closest friend at work, Genevieve. I had called her the day before to make sure Spencer was not going to be back working at the paper and she assured me that he wasn't. She had also heard that he had returned and said that he was taking up a senior role at Metro, one of the big TV networks. She knew I would be upset and made a cutting remark about his lack of manhood to make me feel better. It didn't help, but it was nice that she'd tried.

Before going to my own desk, I went via my editor's office. She briefed me and requested that I follow up Genevieve's story on arranged marriages in my first column that week. 'Why had my own mother not had the foresight to arrange a marriage for me?' I asked myself as I walked to my desk. 'Then I'd have none of these problems and a home may have been part of my dowry.'

I turned on my computer for the first time in nearly a month. My inbox was going to be full and I had to clear it out before I could start writing. I needed to focus and do as much as I could on the column early, so the editor could sign off on it and so I wasn't still sitting there frantically writing on deadline.

I scrolled through my inbox and found that 90 per cent of the emails were media releases. When I got to the bottom of the inbox, there, in bold type, was an email from Spencer, written two weeks earlier. My heart started racing.

From: Spencer Lee
Sent: Monday, 20 December 5:06 PM
To: Maggie Rose
Subject: Home

Hi Maggie,

I know it's been a while, but I thought I should let you know I'm moving back from Tokyo. I've been offered a job at Metro.

I just wanted to tell you I was coming back in case we ran into each other or something.

I hope you're well. Maybe we can have a coffee sometime, as friends?

Merry Christmas,
Spencer

As friends! As if! What was he thinking? Was this some kind of sick joke? I took a deep breath and deleted the email. I was not going to let him back into my life. It hurt too much just seeing his name. It was over and I was getting on with my life.

My heart was pounding and to take my mind off Spencer I went to the kitchen to make myself a coffee — though caffeine is probably not the best idea when mid panic-attack — where Janice, my old boss, also happened to be making herself a cuppa.

When I had worked under Janice, she had done her best to make my life hell and we had never gotten along. Although we had buried the hatchet, so to speak, a few years earlier when she had been integral to my being promoted to the crime desk and getting a weekly blog, I still did not trust her. One minute she was on a power trip, and the next she could turn around and be sweet as pie. I was sure she would be leading the charge in thinking I was not experienced enough to now have my own column.

On top of this, Janice was now the website editor, and on days when I had completed my column and filed it with the paper, I also had to send a soft copy to Janice for the website. As she was not my number one fan, I was never overly happy about letting her see the columns before they appeared in the paper. I wouldn't say I had a lot of creative control when it came to writing my subsequent blogs, either. Although she was no longer able to boss me around on a day-to-day basis like she had in the past, she still had the authority to make things difficult for me when she wanted to.

'Maggie, I want to see a copy of today's column on my desk by 3 pm so I can promote the blog for tomorrow', Janice bluntly said, without even so much as a 'Welcome back, Maggie'. She continued, 'I'll need you to do this every Monday and Thursday from now on, so you'd better get cracking.' It was exactly the kind of one-way 'conversation' I was used to with her.

'No problem. I'll get onto to it right away.'

'Oh, and I heard Spencer's back. That must be tough. Let me know if you need a shoulder', she called back to me, dripping with sarcasm, as she walked back to her desk.

Janice was the only one of Spencer's friends I never liked. She had been my boss when he and I had started going out and she made it clear that she did not think I was good enough for him. For a while before we got together I thought Janice and Spencer were having an office romance themselves, but when Spencer and I started dating I found out that there had actually never been anything between them. Janice had her moments of trying to be nice to me, but she had let me know that she thought it was for the best when Spencer went to Japan. I had never understood how she could be so hot and cold.

***

The first two weeks back at work went by in a blur. The job was high-stress but the editor seemed happy with what I was producing. Janice continued to crack the whip and I continued to perform. A little tug of war in the workplace was just what I needed to keep me on my toes and stop myself thinking about anything not conducive to having a healthy relationship with my own thoughts.

My first date with Alex ended the same way as our plane journey—with a tipsy kiss. It was after a great dinner, though, and I had behaved in a far more civilised way than during our plane rendezvous, which I was still cringing about when we met up again.

After dinner, he asked me back to his place for the night and I said no. He was just about to head off to work in the UK and Europe for a few weeks and I thought it best to protect myself in case I became one of those crazed women who sleeps with someone on the first date and then can't stop herself making a play for the man, even if she isn't quite sure that she really wants to be with him.

However, when Alex asked if I wanted to see him when he got back, I had surprised myself by saying yes. I was being extremely shallow, but he was dead gorgeous, nice and a diversion from Spencer's return. And even though I was sure I didn't want a relationship, I enjoyed hanging out with him.

As he was kissing me goodnight outside my apartment, he told me he was now a hero among his friends for picking up on a plane; something he said many had tried and failed at before.

'That's embarrassing. They must think I'm pretty easy. What are they going to think when you tell them we actually saw each other outside a plane and I sent you home? Won't you lose a bit of street cred?'

'I think you're worth losing some street cred over. I knew I was on to a good thing as soon as I spotted you in the exit row.'

Eliza was right, he was suave.

Work and Alex had also kept my thoughts far away from the idea of buying a home. It was Eliza who brought it up with me over dinner at her and Tom's place in late January. I could feel a lecture coming on as soon as dinner was over. Eliza straightened herself up in her chair and put on her barrister face, which usually signalled some sort of cross-examination.

'Okay, Maggie—Tom and I have been thinking. It's definitely time you started seriously thinking about buying some property. You are earning a good wage now and I know how much you have saved because I looked at a bank statement you left lying around the last time I was at your house. $34 500 is a lot of money.'

'Right. Of course. I have no privacy. And it's currently $30 750, actually. I spent a few thousand on my trip to New York.'

I know most people would have been rather upset if a friend had gone through their mail, but I couldn't get too angry with her for looking at a letter that had probably been sitting open on my kitchen bench. Eliza had taken me in a few years back when I went through my own version of the global financial crisis and she had helped me get back on my feet. I knew she wouldn't have looked on purpose.

'And I know Spencer's back', she said, completely ignoring me, 'and that will be secretly killing you. But what better way to get back at the man who left you for Asia, than to be a fabulous home owner?'

'I really don't think a bank will lend me the money. I'm pretty sure I have a permanent black mark against my name after my years of carefree insolence. And just to set the record straight, I was the one who broke up with Spencer. I'm fine.'

'There are plenty of ways to get around that', Eliza said, referring to the loan and ignoring my statement about Spencer. 'You are just throwing good money away, renting when you could own. Just go online and enter your financials into one of those mortgage calculators that banks have these days.'

When I got home, I took her advice and decided to see how much borrowing power I had. I went online to my bank's website to use the mortgage calculator. As I had a little over $30 000 in the bank, I wanted to see how much it would cost me to borrow another $420 000 to purchase a $450 000 house. The website said I needed a minimum of 10 per cent for the deposit, which would mean I needed another $15 000 for a $450 000 property. I put the figures in for a $420 000 loan amount, anyway.

I had to check a series of boxes. I had to say whether I was to be the owner–occupier or if it was to be an investment property. I had to choose between several types of fixed and variable loans, eventually settling on the standard variable rate of 7.36 per cent over 30 years, simply because it was the first choice and I had no idea what all the different types of loans were. The only one I'd heard of was a standard variable rate.

The final piece of information I needed to enter was an interest-only period. I put in two years, for no other reason than that it was the first number that came into my head. I had no idea what I was doing or what half the terms or figures meant. I couldn't be sure, but I assumed that 'interest-only' was to be taken literally—that for the interest-only period I would only be paying off the interest the bank would charge me on the loan. I was getting more confused and annoyed by the minute and when I pressed 'Calculate' I was given a rather rude shock.

Universal Bank Home Loan Summary

Loan amount	$420 000
Interest	7.36 p.a.
Total interest charge	$634 325
Total repayments	**$1 054 325**
Loan term	30 years
Lump sum repayment	N/A
Detailed summary	
Months 1–24	
Loan	Interest only
Repayments	$2576 per month
Months 25–360	
Loan	Fixed interest 7.36%
Repayments	$2955 per month

The Home Loan Summary laid out the future of a $420 000 mortgage and it wasn't pretty. The total of the repayments that I would be paying to the bank over 30 years was more than a million dollars—and this was for only a $420 000 loan! As I suspected, it was going to be virtually impossible to afford a home on my own. For the first two years, the interest-only period, I would need to be able to afford $2576 per month. After two years, the amount would increase to nearly $3000 a month. I supposed that the higher amount meant I would be paying off the actual loan amount plus the interest, rather than just the interest on its own. But I was just guessing about that. Either way, it was a lot of money. I only took home around $4300 per month. I scribbled down my vague budget to see if there was even a slim chance that I could afford this type of loan.

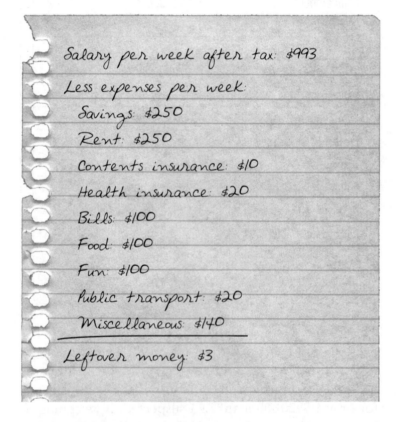

Salary per week after tax: $993
Less expenses per week:
   Savings: $250
   Rent: $250
   Contents insurance: $10
   Health insurance: $20
   Bills: $100
   Food: $100
   Fun: $100
   Public transport: $20
   Miscellaneous: $140
   _____
   Leftover money: $3

I was taking home about $993 a week; of that, I was saving $250 and spending $250 a week on rent. That only left me with less than $500 for everything else in my life, including insurance; food; internet, phone and utilities bills; and socialising. Every spare cent I had went into savings, and a $420 000 interest-only mortgage would cost me about $645 a week. I made some budgetary adjustments.

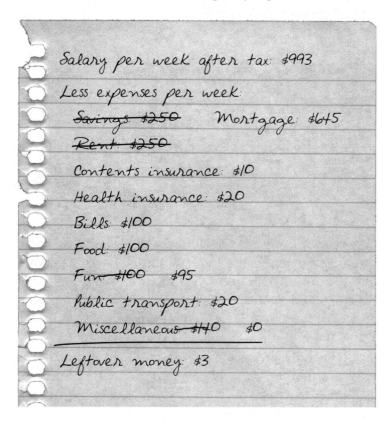

Salary per week after tax: $993

Less expenses per week:

~~Savings $250~~   Mortgage: $645

~~Rent: $250~~

Contents insurance: $10

Health insurance: $20

Bills: $100

Food: $100

Fun ~~$100~~ $95

Public transport: $20

Miscellaneous ~~$110~~ $0

Leftover money: $3

I could see that even though I still wasn't entirely sure what an interest-only loan was, paying off this type of loan would mean I had no money left over. And when I started paying back the full monthly $3000 amount owed to the bank after the 24th month—which would be closer to $750 a week— I would no longer be able to afford the $100 or so that I had allocated to myself each week to have a good time.

Feeling more than a little despondent, I decided to use the real estate search engine to look for houses in Leighton within an actual price range: $350000 to $450000. I wanted at least two bedrooms, but the number of bathrooms wasn't important.

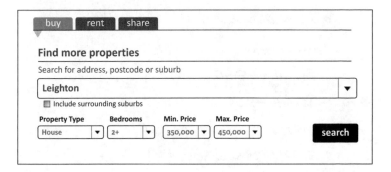

I clicked 'Search' and waited for the screen to load. Nothing came up. Absolutely nothing. There was not a single two-bedroom house for sale in Leighton between $350000 and $450000. I increased the maximum price to $500000 and chose to 'include surrounding suburbs' to see if a wider search yielded greater returns.

The only property for sale in Leighton with that search criteria was a single-fronted, two-bedroom house going for '$500000-plus'—out of my league—however, there was a house in the neighbouring suburb of Parklands with an asking price of $470000. This was promising. Parklands was a little farther out of the city than Leighton, but still within walking distance of the CBD. Although the Parklands house needed a little bit of work, the photos showed that the owners had gone to a lot of effort to present it tastefully. I could see myself living there.

I needed help and I cursed myself for not paying more attention to Eliza when she was buying her first home. I was too busy living it up, living pay cheque to pay cheque and maxing out my credit cards to worry about something 'grown up' like investing my money in property. House-hunting was never even remotely on the radar. Now it was, and I needed answers, but I didn't want to be always relying on Eliza to solve my problems. It was time to take action myself.

When I had been struggling to sort out my finances a few years earlier, Eliza had suggested that I see a financial adviser. The man I saw, Jason, had turned out to be a complete lifesaver. At the time of our first meeting, I had been trying for six months to get myself out of debt, with little success. I hadn't known what to pay off first or how to save. His advice had sorted me out within a few months. I sold my car, paid off all of my credit cards and started putting money away for the future.

Jason not only gave me great advice and put me on the straight and narrow, but he also instilled in me the confidence I needed to know I wasn't a complete loser for not having a clue how to save. He also made me realise I was not alone when it came to being shocking with my money. So I made an appointment to see him the next week in the hope that he would be able to help me on my way to buying my first home.

In the meantime, I hopped back online and registered with the real estate website to receive daily email alerts for new properties. From a brief stint working on the financial desk at the newspaper, I knew that the inner-city property market practically shuts down over Christmas and doesn't really take off again until the New Year, so February was a good time to start looking ... but not necessarily a good time to be buying, as there would be less choice than if the market was in full force. Nevertheless, each day I would receive an email at work and at home, alerting me to the latest two-bedroom properties that had come onto the market in Leighton and its surrounding suburbs.

In the week before I met with Jason, I focused on work and the long-awaited second date with Alex. At my regular Thursday morning radio spot there was a new producer who I had not met before. Her name was Angelica. She introduced herself to me and rather proudly told me she was a 'very' close friend of Janice's. She also bluntly told me I should ask her if I needed help because she had been told I wasn't as experienced as the other journalists from *The City* who also did the slot. Janice strikes again.

Who was this woman and what happened to the other lovely producer who always made me a cup of tea? I wanted to know, but was too scared to ask the waspish woman standing in front of me wearing a perfectly ironed outfit, with matching leather jacket and shoes—in my opinion a look that was almost as bad as double denim.

I was used to Janice being less than human to me, but it was unprofessional of her to have so blatantly gone out of her way to undermine me. We were colleagues and as much as I wanted to defend myself and ask Angelica why the editor would have put me in such a role if I was so 'inexperienced', I loathed confrontations and decided to just do my 20 minutes and get out of there.

Later that afternoon at work, I diligently emailed Janice my column on a breakthrough in breast cancer research at a local university. Her usual email response was a short and simple 'thanks'. However, this time she also asked me whether I had met her good friend Angelica at the radio station. She knew I had, but rather than sending her a rude retort I just responded that yes, I'd met her. What I really wanted to do was tell her exactly what I thought of her and Angelica, and that I didn't appreciate being told I was 'inexperienced'.

The next night was my second official date with Alex. He was back from Europe and had called me to confirm our dinner plans. It was the first week of February and had been a little more than a month since our infamous flight home together.

I snuck out of work an hour early to get ready. We had arranged to meet at a restaurant in town. I knew it was expensive and I wanted to look good even if I wasn't quite ready to accept that I was genuinely excited about seeing him again.

We met at a French bistro in town. Alex came to the restaurant straight from work so, unlike our first meeting and first date where he was dressed in jeans, he was wearing an extremely well-cut suit. He was charm personified and told me he'd been diligently reading my column and my blog online, and said he thought I was very talented. After Angelica's 'inexperienced' comment, Alex's enthusiasm was just what I needed.

I'd only had a couple of brief emails from him while he'd been away, so we talked about his trip—he'd been to conferences in Paris, London, Dublin, Frankfurt and Berlin—and he said he didn't have to go on another work trip for another month. Alex obviously loved his job, but was just as happy talking nonsense, which was a relief because I was not in the mood for serious conversation.

I hadn't been out for almost two weeks and wanted to have a fun night.

'My mother says sometimes she doesn't believe I'm a lawyer and says I must be a spy. What do you think?' he said as we were walking to a bar after dinner.

'There *is* something quite spyish about you. Actually, you have a bit of a Superman quality about you', I flirted back.

'It's the glasses. Chicks dig the specs.'

It wasn't the glasses. He was a tall, broad man and looked really fit and healthy. I, on the other hand, was a more voluptuous design. I liked exercising and tried my hardest to walk for an hour three or four mornings a week, but it did not change the fact that I was a curvy woman. I had long ago come to accept that, apart from having long, blond hair, I was never going to look like Jessica Hart or Elle Macpherson. I still would have liked to lose a few kilos, though.

Yet Alex didn't seem to mind, because he again asked if we could spend the night together, this time at my apartment. And again I had to say no. I liked him, but I wanted to take it really slowly; he had to be content with another kiss goodnight. But just to keep him keen, when he dropped me home in the taxi I leaned over and whispered in his ear, 'Better luck next time'. His laugh told me he loved it.

***

It was good to see Jason again, and his advice was pure and simple. I had to move out of my apartment and into a cheaper place if I was going to save the deposit for a home that year. Not exactly what I wanted to hear.

'Maggie, I'm pumped for you. This is a great step and one you are definitely ready for.' Jason was a total livewire who was possibly the only person alive who could make me excited about finances.

'I can't believe how far you've come, Maggie. I'm really proud of you', he said when I handed him my latest statement showing I had $31 000 in savings. I told him I knew that was my starting point, but wanted to be a home owner as quickly as possible. I also said I was looking at $450 000 homes.

His response was not what I expected.

'Slow down, Maggie. You have still got a long way to go and a lot to learn. Yes, you feel ready to buy a home but you don't have nearly enough money yet.'

'How much will I need?'

'I'll have to work all that out for you, but on a $65 000 salary and with 30 grand in the bank, you can't afford a loan on a $450 000 house. I can tell you that much without a calculator.'

I told him I had put my financial details into the Universal Bank's home loan calculator and I made just enough to cover the mortgage repayments if I borrowed $420 000 of the cost of a house…at least for the first two years.

'That's just the tip of the iceberg. Look, I'm not trying to burst your bubble or anything, but buying a home is not just about having the 10 per cent deposit. There are thousands of dollars in extra costs that you have to consider and we need to get you saving so you have as much money as possible in the bank when it comes time to buy.'

He then asked me if there was any chance my parents were going to help me out financially, how much rent I was paying and what I was prepared to sacrifice in order to save.

I hadn't thought about asking my parents for money. I'm sure they would have lent me money if I'd asked, but I wanted to do the whole house thing without them. I'd never owned anything except for a few nice pieces of furniture and a car, and I wanted to see if it was possible for me to buy a house alone. As for the sacrifices, I wasn't quite sure how far I was willing to go.

'I'm paying $250 a week in rent and saving $250. The rest just goes on bills and going out.'

'Okay, I'm going to give you a couple of scenarios here. If you stay where you are and continue saving the $250 a week, you will have a $45 000 in a little over a year. If you moved back home with your parents, rent-free, and saved $500 a week, you'd have the money in six months.'

'There is no way I'm moving home with my mum and dad. I'm 32 years old and I haven't lived at home in a decade. I love them dearly, but I'd drive them mad. And vice versa.'

'I'm just putting options out there. So what about moving into a share house? If you could find a place where you were paying less rent, you would be in a much better financial position in a shorter time.'

I started to feel panicky. I loved living on my own and the idea of going back to share-house living was not ideal. I didn't want to move out of my apartment. I had slaved to get there and I didn't think I could go back to sharing a bathroom. I knew he was right, though. While I was sitting there sweating, Jason had the calculator out and was doing more sums.

'This is what I think you need to do to start with. Think about living with your parents. Otherwise, it's now

February, and if you move into a place where you're paying $125 a week and can start saving $375 a week, you will have another $9750 saved by August. With the government's $7000 first home owner grant, that will take your savings to around $48000 to put towards your first home.'

I only vaguely knew what the first home owner grant was, but I couldn't focus on that. All I could think was that, unfortunately, he was right about my living arrangements. The first time I had gone to see Jason I had fought with him when he told me to sell my car, but it had ultimately been the best decision I made as it had allowed me to be debt-free for the first time in my adult life. If I really wanted a home, sacrifices had to be made.

'I'm going to let you go and have a think about all of this and in a few weeks you can give me a call and we'll make a time to meet again. I'll create a new budget to get you on your way. We'll also sit down and discuss everything you need to know about buying real estate. In the meantime, try to put away an extra $50 a week.'

I was already saving $250 week. $300 plus my rent was going to be a stretch.

***

The property alerts started streaming into my inbox as the property market started gearing up for the year, and I found myself looking forward to logging on to my computer at work and at home just to see what had come up for sale. A recent property boom had made every second home-owner think they could make a killing if they put their house on the market. It also meant people were also asking for a lot more for a lot less. Buying in Leighton was increasingly looking like a dream, as prices seemed to rise on a weekly basis. But I wasn't going to worry about it until I had put some serious money aside.

I went and saw my parents and told them that Jason had suggested I move in with them. The look of horror on my dad's face said it all. Mum said I was welcome to stay but I quickly told them I had no intention of doing so — much to the relief of my father, whose face had gone as white as a ghost.

Arriving home one night after work, I sat at my kitchen table and thought about the reality of moving into a share house. My lease was coming up for renewal very soon, so if I was going to move out, this was the time to do it. But I loved living on my own, and if I was going to share there were a few conditions on which I was not willing to budge. Firstly, I didn't want to live with strangers and, secondly, I definitely didn't want to share a bathroom with some pimple-faced boy still at university.

None of my friends had spare rooms, but I thought someone at work might have a friend in need of a housemate. Ten days after that first meeting with Jason, I put up a notice at work asking if anyone needed a roommate. On Wednesday, Julia, one of the sports reporters, told me her flatmate was moving out of her place in three weeks and I was welcome to the room.

Julia and I had been cadet journalists together and still got on well. She lived in a two-bedroom townhouse in Charles, a suburb on the other side of the city from Leighton but still close to work. Julia said she shared one bedroom with her boyfriend, James, and that the rent on the other bedroom was $150 a week, including utilities. I'd also have my own bathroom! It was an offer too good to refuse. I made a mental note of how much money I would be saving and said yes before even seeing her place. I went back to my desk and called my real estate agent to give a month's notice on my flat and, to make the most of living alone, I invited Alex around for dinner on Friday night.

Each week at my radio slot Angelica made it increasingly clear that she didn't like me and I had no idea why; I was completely inconsequential to her life. Angelica was the type of woman I would have loved to be when I was about 16 years old. Tall, thin and full of confidence, she looked and acted like an overly ambitious head girl. She had incredible long, blond curly hair and a waist the size of Kate Moss', despite being close to six foot tall. My own hair was long and blond, but it didn't bounce like hers did.

While waiting to go on air that week I overheard her talking to her boyfriend on her phone, gloating about her time at Harvard University. I was impressed and it didn't surprise me; Angelica was obviously an overachiever. It just made me like her even less, though, and I felt genuine pity for the poor man she had lured into her spindly clutches.

What had previously been an enjoyable weekly outing to the radio studio was fast turning into a major pain in the bum. Angelica seemed to know a lot about me and I knew nothing about her. Janice was obviously on a mission to make my life as uncomfortable as possible, and Angelica was her accomplice. A brief thought of quitting the radio slot was quickly halted by Eliza and Fran that night over a simple dinner at my place.

'Are you crazy? You can't let some skinny idiot push you around', Eliza said.

'And besides, Maggie, you need the money to buy a house', Fran said.

'You're right. I thought I was too old to be bullied. I feel like I'm back in high school. Angelica and Janice think they are the cool kids. I just want to be left alone.'

'They're just jealous of you because you're really beautiful and have your own column', the ever-so-sweet Fran told me.

'Thanks, Franny, but Janice is the editor of the website and is "above" me at work, and Angelica is certainly *not* intimidated by me.'

'Next time Angelica's rude, just politely ask her what the hell her problem is. You need that job', the ever-straightforward Eliza said.

Date three with Alex went according to plan. I cooked him a romantic French dinner and he continued to make me laugh. He stayed the night and when I woke up the next morning I was happy for him to be there. It was the first time in a long time that I had a crush on someone. Over the next fortnight, Alex stayed a further four times. And as I packed up my apartment and prepared to move in with Julia and James, he invited me to his bachelor pad in town.

Alex lived in a huge apartment at the southern end of the CBD. It must have been worth a fortune. It had been obvious to me already that Alex was successful at his job—he was a partner at his law firm and he did so much international travel that they must value him—but his apartment confirmed his success. He owned the penthouse of an early 20th-century building! Not bad for a scruffy-looking 36-year-old who liked to wear sneakers, jeans and t-shirts.

At the beginning of March he helped me move out of my apartment. I took a day of leave and hired a truck, and we moved most of my belongings into my parents' garage, and my bed, desk, clothes and a few bookshelves to the room in my new house. Julia and James' house was fully furnished, so none of my communal furniture or kitchenware was needed.

A few days after he helped me move, Alex went to work at his firm's New York office for a month. I was miserable after he left. Adding to my misery was that my new place was tiny and in the first days I barely felt comfortable leaving my bedroom.

Max called to tell me that the next day was auction day for the decrepit house at the end of my old street in Leighton, and that he was going to take a look. So on the first Saturday after I moved into my new home I found myself on the train going back to my old neighbourhood, to my first ever auction. Not to bid, just to take a look.

Max and Jem picked me up at the station in Leighton at 9.30 am, and we went out for brunch before the auction later that morning. Max had decided he was going to be my real estate mentor for the day, and pulled out the newspaper to show me how he had found a house for Jem and himself.

'Every Saturday morning we would get up early, get the papers and plan out the day around the houses we wanted to inspect, and the auctions we wanted to watch', he said.

'I don't have a car so it's going to be hard for me to get around', I replied.

'Just pick two neighbouring suburbs and spend the day looking, then.'

'And we can come with you to some', Jem added.

We arrived in my old street and I felt a pang for the life I had left behind just a few days earlier. Julia's place just didn't feel like home yet.

There were more than a hundred people waiting out the front of the broken-down old house. Max said it was because land in Leighton was so valuable and people were desperate to buy in the area. We walked through the home and I felt sad for the family. The flyer said it was the home's first offering in 60 years. 'The old man must have brought up his family in the house', I said aloud, but to myself.

We found a spot under a tree across the road from the house to watch the auctioneer do his thing. He started with the legalities of the sale and then started spruiking the property's potential. Just as he was about to ask for bids, I spotted Angelica in the crowd. A man stood beside her, holding her hand, so I moved to get a better view of her and see what her boyfriend looked like. Angelica took a step to one side and then I saw the face of the man she was with. Spencer. I started to feel ill but at the same time I couldn't look away. There was *my* Spencer, just 15 metres away. And he was with *her*. And they were at an auction *together*.

Jem saw me waver and looked up just as Spencer and Angelica turned and spotted us. I felt the colour draining from my face and thought I might actually be sick. Jem stood in front of me to shield me but Spencer was already walking over.

'This cannot be happening', I said to Jem as Spencer fast approached us with Angelica close behind him.

'You'll be okay, honey. You're a tough cookie. Just don't overreact; he's not worth it', Jem said through clenched teeth as they moved in for the kill.

'Maggie, hi', Spencer said.

'Wow, good to see you', I lied. 'When did you get back?' He looked the same. My heart broke all over again and I had an overwhelming urge to lean forward and kiss him.

Before he had a chance to continue, Angelica cut in and introduced herself to Max and Jem as Spencer's girlfriend. Spencer, Jem and I stood there awkwardly while Angelica rabbitted on about what a coincidence it was that we were all at the same auction. My world was spinning around. What had I done to deserve this? Of all the people who could have been the new girlfriend of my ex-boyfriend who broke my heart, why did it have to be Angelica, a woman who clearly hated me? And of all the places to look for a house to buy together, why did it have to be Leighton? How could these terrible coincidences be happening to me?

Everything suddenly came to a grinding halt as I heard the auctioneer yell out, 'First call, second call, third and final call...SOLD for $895000!' That was double what I thought I could afford. Whoa. This was all too overwhelming and I needed to get out of there. I politely said goodbye to Spencer and Angelica, grabbed my bag and walked towards Max's car. I didn't have to say anything to him or Jem; they knew I wanted to get away, *tout suite.*

I almost ran to the car and Max beeped it open so I could jump straight in. As soon as we had pulled out onto the road I started sobbing and didn't stop until the car pulled into my driveway, when I realised they had driven me all the way home. But I didn't want to go inside. I didn't want to be in a place that didn't feel like home.

'Can you drop me off at Eliza's place? I'm sorry for being a pain; I just really don't want to be here tonight.'

Lessons learned

- Don't get drunk on planes.
- A good real estate search engine is a handy resource when house-hunting.
- Work out a basic budget so you can be realistic about how much money you have to spend each week.
- Going to see a financial adviser can be a great way to get your finances in shape.
- Do your research so that you don't turn up to auctions in suburbs you clearly can't afford.

PART II

Reality check

April to June

Dream home: a two-bedroom, two-bathroom house, in need of a lick of paint to get it up to Home Beautiful standard, situated in or near Leighton and going for around $450000

Savings: $33500

Deposit needed: about $45 000?

Happiness: what's that?

After the shock of seeing Spencer I went into a self-imposed hiatus. It was time to hunker down and focus on buying a home.

It's always a revolting feeling the first time you run into someone you used to love after a break-up. It's the kind of moment you want to have at least a month to prepare for so you can get your hair blow-waved, lose that last pesky five kilograms and be in your sexiest 'just thrown on' outfit. As well as looking good, you also want to be the maestro orchestrating every move of the meeting. Clearly that didn't happen for me.

I knew I couldn't avoid seeing him forever, but for him to be with Angelica, of all people, was just downright depressing. I mean, I had to see the woman at the radio station each week. At least it explained why she was rude to me. There was no doubt she knew I was Spencer's ex and there was no doubt she had loved seeing me squirm at the auction as she told Jem, Max and me that she was his girlfriend.

I avoided eye contact with Angelica in the weeks afterwards. It was the only way I could guarantee not having an on-air meltdown in front of her and Darren the radio host. My habit had always been to arrive at the studio with at least 10 minutes to spare before my spot, but I started arriving only five minutes early. It was the best idea I could come up with to avoid her. The thought of having to see her perfect hair and her giraffe-like legs clad in skin-tight jeans was enough to make my blood boil. Sometimes I could see her readying herself to come over and talk to me, and to discourage her from approaching I'd grab my phone and pretend to be intently texting someone.

Apart from all the Angelica nonsense, there were some positive things happening in my life. I had saved a further $2750 in the three months since coming home from New York and by mid-April the decision to move in with Julia and James was paying off—even if I was a little miserable and their place sometimes felt like it was the size of a mouse hole. I now had $33500 and my deposit was only months away from being ready to go. Or so I thought.

The home alerts kept coming in via email, but none of the houses were within my price range, nor were they in Leighton. Logging onto my computer was still my favourite part of the day, though, because I had full faith that one morning the perfect home would flash up on my screen.

I still had quite a way to go financially before I could do any serious house-hunting, but I decided to follow Max's advice and start looking at houses on the weekends to see what was around and get the feel of the auction scene. Although I had specifically requested home alerts for Leighton, I had also chosen the option to receive alerts for surrounding suburbs, so most of the houses that were sent to my inbox—and that were in my price range!—were in Parklands and Monovale, the two suburbs to the north of Leighton. I liked them both; they were within walking distance to work and were on the same train line as Leighton, and they had some lovely tree-lined streets similar to Leighton. My heart was still set on Leighton, but I knew I had to be a little flexible or I would be looking forever.

The first Saturday I went house-hunting out on my own was more difficult than I expected. Just as Max had said I should, I mapped out a plan to inspect a couple of houses and watch a few auctions in my chosen suburbs. Without a car, the quickest way for me to get to each place was by bike, so I dusted off the helmet and planned to ride to each of the inspections and auctions. I made a map and marked the spots. If I arrived at the first inspection in Parklands on time, I could allow myself 10 minutes to inspect the house, then would have a leisurely 20 minutes to get to the next house only a few blocks away. Allowing 10 minutes to see that house, I would then have another 20 minutes to ride over to an auction for a house at the opposite end of Parklands. Depending on how long the auction took, I would then have to rush to get to another auction in Leighton. I was pretty fit; that plan would be no problem at all.

- 10 am—Inspection: 15 Union St. Parklands
- 10.30 am—Inspection: 99 Carlisle Gve, Parklands
- 11 am—Auction: 197 Stanley St. Parklands
- 11.30 am—Auction: 72 Best St. Leighton

But I was wrong. I rode across town to Parklands thinking I had plenty of time to see the first open for inspection. Unfortunately, I had totally underestimated how long the ride would take and when I arrived at the Union Street home the inspection was already over. It was then that I realised I had left my map at home and had no idea where the next house was located. I thought it was around the corner but when I went to ask a woman on the street for directions she said it was a good 15-minute ride away.

Hot-footing it across the suburb with the woman's directions only partially memorised, I quickly got lost and ended up close to my old street in Leighton. I didn't have time to make the inspection and I was worried I would get lost again if I turned around and tried to make the Parklands auction, so I gave up and decided to just go to the Leighton auction and be done with it. I knew how to get there from my old street without a map.

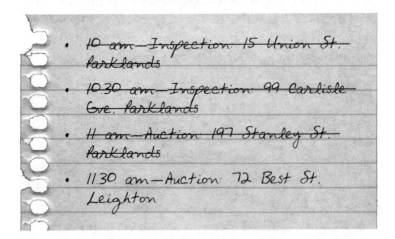

* 10 am—Inspection: 15 Union St, Parklands
* 10.30 am—Inspection: 99 Carlisle Ave, Parklands
* 11 am—Auction: 197 Stanley St, Parklands
* 11.30 am—Auction: 72 Best St, Leighton

I had some time to kill so I sat down and had a coffee at my old local café. For the first time in more than a month, I caught my breath and had time to think about what I was doing. I hadn't been out in weeks and had spent almost every weekend since I had run into Spencer hibernating in my new home. Alex was still away and had told me in an email a few days beforehand that his New York trip had been extended.

When did I stop having a good time? I needed a night out and I needed it fast. The thought of a third Saturday night in a row at home with Julia and James was wearing thin.

While I waited for my coffee, I rang Fran, Tim and Genevieve and organised to go out for dinner. I had budgeted for $100 a week to have a good time, so I wasn't going to eat into my savings by going out for one night. Besides, at my current bicycle-powered house-hunting rate it would be a long time before I'd need any sort of deposit, anyway!

I turned up to the Leighton auction with 10 minutes to spare, locked my bike to a tree and walked through the house with the other dozen people already inside inspecting it. The house was small and with all the people jostling to inspect the wardrobes, bathroom and tiny bedrooms it felt as though I was walking through a packed dollhouse. Again, it was not a house I could afford—the vendors were asking for more than $550 000—but it was probably the closest I was going to get to a place in Leighton, and I wanted to actually watch an auction rather than be shocked into oblivion as I had been at the last one I attended.

By the time I fought my way back out onto the street, there were at least 50 people standing along the road. And in the five minutes that I stood outside waiting for the auction to begin, another 20 people had joined the crowd. I knew the market was flourishing, but I didn't think there would be so many people at the auctions. Had I missed something extraordinary about that house?

The crowd was filled with young couples presumably looking for their first home, as well as some older couples, men and women standing on their own (like me) and people who were clearly neighbours from the street, having a stickybeak.

A man in a suit walked out the front gate and turned to the crowd. 'My name is Henry Jones', he said. 'On behalf of Leighton Quality Real Estate, I'll be your auctioneer today.'

He then went on to talk about the contract of sale, which he said had been available for interested parties to see inside the house. I didn't see it anywhere, and wondered whether anyone else had, given the number of people inside the house with me.

'Ladies and gentlemen', he said. 'Before we start the auction I need to tell you I will accept bids of $1000, $2000, $5000 and $10000. No bids will be accepted if they are less than the amount called for by the auctioneer. No bids shall be retracted. I am entitled to make bids on behalf of the vendor and the highest non-vendor bid shall be the successful bidder.'

The auctioneer sounded to me like he was talking crazy. Wasn't the vendor the person selling the house? So if the auctioneer made a bid on behalf of the vendor, wouldn't that mean the vendor was bidding to buy their own house? It didn't make sense, and I clearly had no idea what this auction caper was all about. Where was Max when I needed him?

'Now, this home is all about location, location, location', the auctioneer continued. 'This may not be the best home in Leighton, but it is a blue-chip position — you will struggle to find a better spot in the area. It needs major cosmetic surgery, but the vendors have council-approved plans to renovate. You are not going to get a better house in Leighton for this price.'

The auctioneer was blatantly lying, as I knew there were far better streets and houses in the area. Not only was the house for auction near a main freeway that was very noisy at all times of the day and night, but there was a large factory at the end of the street and it was at least a 20-minute walk from the train station. I wouldn't have minded living there if I could have afforded it, but to say it was a blue-chip location was a bit far-fetched — even if it was in Leighton.

The auctioneer kept talking. 'I've sent out more than 50 contracts to interested parties this week for prior viewing and I can see a fair few of those parties here today, so let's get started. Are there any questions?'

The crowd was silent except for a small child asking his mother for water.

'Right. Do I have an opening bid?'

He waited. No-one made a bid, so the agent kept spruiking the house's potential and the location before he tried again.

'Can I have a starting bid of $500 000?'

Again, no-one said a word.

The agent kept talking — I was impressed by his verbosity — and out of nowhere he said, '$500 000. Is that a bid for $500 000, madam?'

I looked around and could see a young couple standing on my right. The woman was nodding her head at the auctioneer. They looked nervous and it was pretty easy to tell that, like me, they were new to the auction scene.

'Yes, we have a bid for $500 000. Can I see a hand for $510 000? Can I hear $510 000?'

There was a 30-second silence before a man put up his hand and bid for $510 000. The first bidder turned to her partner and whispered in his ear before adding another $10 000 to take it to $520 000. The second bidder swiftly put in another $10 000 offer.

The auctioneer asked for further bids, but none were forthcoming. He told the crowd it was going once for $530 000, then twice.

Everyone in the crowd seemed to be holding their collective breaths. The young couple huddled together and looked as though they were trying to figure out their next move, while their opponent stared straight at the agent. The bidding seemed to have really stopped — this was going to be it!

'I'm going to let you all know that the house is now *officially* on the market', said the auctioneer.

On the market? I thought it had been 'on the market' the entire time, but apparently the bidding had to get to a certain price before the house could be declared 'for sale'. Who knew?

Suddenly, there was a flurry of bids. I couldn't believe it; the first and second bidders were still in the game, but another man and a woman had jumped in as well. A quick fire of only six bids pushed the price up to $620 000!

I decided to move towards the front and off to the side, where I could watch the crowd rather than looking at the auctioneer. I really wanted to see how the crowd would react when the house was sold, and who it was sold to.

I could see a man slowly making his way through the crowd; he was wearing a trench coat and was probably in his early 50s. I had noticed him leaning on the fence opposite the house before the auction began, but now he had moved right into the middle of the gathering.

The highest bidder at that stage was a man in his 60s standing with two women, who I assumed were his wife and daughter. He looked quite relaxed, but by the way his daughter was biting her nails and nervously looking around, it was also easy to assume he was trying to buy the house for her.

'At $620000, do I hear another offer?' the agent asked.

I scanned the crowd. The man in the trench coat had moved to the front, directly to the left of the auctioneer. I assumed that, like me, he wanted to get a better view of the action.

Just as the auctioneer was about to say 'sold at $620000' — $70000 above the advertised price! — Trench Coat chimed in with a bid.

'That's $625000, ladies and gentleman, to the man in the tan coat. Can I hear another $1000?'

The previous bidder, who I had thought was a shoo-in to win, turned to his wife and daughter. His wife nodded and the man raised his hand to shoulder level and added another $1000.

Trench Coat quickly counterbid another $1000. His opponent again looked at his wife for confirmation to make another offer, but she was shaking her head.

It was an amazing show. The crowd was captivated and Trench Coat's tactics had blown the other bidders out of the water. Coming in at the last moment seemed to be a smart move. Everyone else had exhausted their funds and Trench Coat had been able to control how much money he was putting in. Well, at least that's what he seemed to be doing, to my uninitiated eye.

Finally the agent called out, 'Sold to this gentleman for $627000. Congratulations, sir!'

It felt like such a relief to hear him say 'sold'—I hadn't realised, but I'd been clenching my jaw with the tension.

I walked back to my bike realising I had a long way to go before I was going to be a winning bidder myself. The property market was pulsing and my first thoughts of buying in Leighton were quashed. If a rundown two-bedroom cottage was being sold for almost $630000, I was never going to be in with a chance. For a $630000 mortgage, I would need at least another $30000 for a deposit, and there was no way I'd be able to make the repayments on my salary—I'd have to get a third job for that!

Over dinner, I gave Fran, Genevieve, Tim and his girl-friend, Yvette, the rundown of the auction. We went to a cheap and cheerful restaurant in the city. The nights were still warm and we were able to get a table outside on the street. After all my angst about Spencer and feeling low about the house, it was great to sit down, have a drink and relax.

Fran was excited because she had just met a new guy who she was going out with the next night. Fran worked in marketing for a fashion label. She was the sweetest woman I had ever had the pleasure of meeting. We had become friends at university and had stayed friends ever since. It had been years since she had met anyone she had really been interested in, so it was nice to see her excited.

It was also great to see Genevieve, as I hadn't seen her outside the newsroom since the evening after I'd seen Spencer and Angelica at the auction—that night, Eliza had held an emergency 'Maggie Meltdown' session at her place, which involved vodka and pizza; lots of both. Genevieve and I had been friends at work for years. She was the only person I could completely trust in the office and she made me laugh like no-one else could.

Like Fran and myself, Genevieve was unlucky in love. This was despite her having the most kick-arse Scottish accent I'd ever heard, as well as gorgeous, sparkling green eyes and killer legs. She also did a mean Janice impersonation that sent me into fits of laughter whenever she turned it on for me—usually in an attempt to make me feel better about something Janice had said or done to me.

As I told them all about my disastrous day looking at houses, we inevitably got talking about Spencer and Angelica.

'I still can't believe you ran into them like that. What are the odds?' Fran said.

'Neither can I', I replied. 'Why is he going out with her? And now they're buying a house together? It's bizarre. If it was someone remotely nice, I could understand it. But she's awful; absolutely awful. And the worst thing is that she seems to derive a lot of pleasure from knowing she's now with my ex-boyfriend.'

'Yeah, that's just weird', Genevieve said.

'And what's even weirder is that she has long blond hair, just like you', chimed Fran with a smirk. 'Do you think he's trying to recreate something with her that he no longer has with you? Oh, wait! Do you think maybe he loved your hair just as much as you do?' She cracked up. I look after my hair and I still like to get it blow-waved every week. Fran loved taking the mickey out of my obsession with my hair.

'Yeah, Fran. Angelica is my clone. That's why we're *both* stick figures who could be on any European catwalk',

I laughed. And with my tongue firmly in my cheek, I added, 'You know, come to think of it, I often wondered why he always asked if he could brush my hair for me. It creeped me out.'

To be fair to Spencer, he had never actually asked to brush my hair, but this made us all crack up. I loved my friends for helping me make light of a distressing subject and knowing that it was exactly what I needed. I promised myself to make more of an effort to catch up with them than I had been. I may have been saving, but I wasn't a nun.

Dinner turned into drinks at a local bar and at 1 am Genevieve, Fran and I said goodbye to Tim and Yvette. We then headed to a club in the city to dance. By 2.30 am I was exhausted and needed bed.

When I got home I pulled out my phone to put it on the charger and saw that I had missed a call from Alex. He had left a message saying he was, finally, back in town and wanted to take me out for dinner. My heart skipped a beat. He wasn't great at keeping in contact when he was away and I had been so busy that it wasn't until he contacted me that I realised I'd really missed hanging out with him. Things were looking up for the first time in weeks.

When Alex took me out for a romantic dinner the next week at a restaurant near his apartment, he presented me with some perfume and a beautiful one-off print from a famous New York gallery. He was almost too good to be true. In fact, apart from the lack of contact while he was away, I couldn't really fault him. He made me feel great about myself. He was also going to be home for at least two months and told me he intended to spend most of it with me. Bliss!

Alex had offered to go and see some houses with me that Saturday. I had been planning to ride my bike around town again, but Alex's offer was great on two counts: I got to hang out with him for the whole day and I didn't have to ride.

We arrived at the first house to the familiar scene of too many people in too small a space. In the few weeks I had been looking at houses I had seen many of the same people over and over again at every inspection and auction I'd been to. I obviously wasn't alone in looking for a reasonably priced house in the inner northern suburbs. I just hoped it didn't mean I would run into Angelica and Spencer again.

But maybe I wouldn't see them again because they'd already bought a place. So which would be worse — seeing them or not seeing them? I started imagining them cosied up in their beautifully decorated lounge room ... In the middle of my daydream about Spencer and Angelica's happy home, I noticed Alex was talking and I tuned back in.

'—you really need to do you research.'

I smiled as if I'd been listening the whole time, and swiftly changed the subject. 'When did you buy your apartment, Alex?'

'I actually bought my first house way out in the suburbs when I was 28, and five years later I sold it to buy the apartment I live in now.'

'Did you make much money on it?'

'I made \$300 000 in five years and I only renovated the bathroom. To be honest, though, it was in a great area and I had a bit of luck by selling it just as the property boom was really moving. Also, being in the property game has given me a bit of knowhow. My agent thinks my apartment has already gone up a lot since I bought it a year ago and I'll make at least $200 000 again when I sell in a few years.

'Have you thought about buying an apartment instead of a house, Maggie? There's a nice one going in my building', Alex said jokingly.

'Are you asking me to move in with you?' I teased.

'No, seriously. There's a great apartment for sale in my building. It only has one bedroom but there's only one of you', Alex said, ignoring my joke. 'I know you have your heart set on a house, but I know a little bit about the real estate game and I think an apartment is a good investment.'

'But will it make me as much money as owning land?'

'It depends. In the long-run maybe not, but for the short-term it's an excellent and affordable option. And you can definitely afford a modern apartment.'

He had some valid points, but I wanted a house and I was sure that there was not much Alex or anyone could say to convince me otherwise.

We went outside to watch the auction and I again picked a spot close to the front so we could turn and see what was going on in the crowd. I had told Alex about the man wearing the trench coat I'd seen swoop in at the last auction I'd been to and I wanted to see if someone else would use the same tactic.

But this time it was a totally different scenario. Not a single person bid. After a while, the auctioneer said he needed to speak with the owners, and went inside the house.

'What's going on?' I asked Alex.

'He's going inside to check that he can put in a vendor bid.'

'What exactly is a vendor bid? I've heard of them but haven't seen one used at an auction yet.'

'It's when the auctioneer puts in a bid on behalf of the owner. It can be used in a variety of ways before and during an auction. It's often used to try to keep an auction moving, but I assume this time he wants to use it to get the auction going.'

'But if no-one's bidding, doesn't that mean no-one wants the house?'

'Ah, Maggie, you have so much to learn', he said while playfully ruffling my hair. 'This happens all the time. Sometimes people don't want to bid because they want to wait to see what happens. This is a pretty good place and the market is still riding high, so I doubt there won't be a bid.'

And he was right. The agent walked out and made a vendor bid of $570 000. This was $30 000 more than the advertised price of $540 000. It took a further two minutes, which felt like an hour in auction time, but someone in the crowd finally made a bid.

An older man put in an offer of $575 000. As usual, I assumed the game was up and the man was a sure-thing to win, but when the agent said the house was still not on the market, the crowd went silent. After a few minutes of no bids, the auctioneer said the house was passed in.

'What's going on?' I asked Alex again. My naivety was beginning to sound like a broken record.

'The house has been passed in. That means the bidding didn't get to the reserve, or minimum, price the sellers wanted.'

'But they put in a vendor's bid, so shouldn't that be the minimum price they want?'

'You'd think so, but that's not how it works. A vendor can put in a bid of any amount. In this case the vendor's bid was used to get the auction started—even though it didn't really work!—but that doesn't automatically mean the vendor would have bid their reserve price. But, see, the man who put in the last bid is going inside to negotiate.'

I watched the man walk into the house with the agent. Alex explained that whoever had made the highest bid when a house was passed in was entitled to go inside and negotiate with the owners.

I don't know why I'd always assumed that every house that went up for auction got sold. I checked the real estate sales results in the paper the next day and it said the house was passed in. The man obviously wasn't able to negotiate a winning price.

***

I went to see Jason at the end of April. I knew he would have a new budget ready for me, and although I wasn't particularly looking forward to it, I knew it was necessary. Jason had put me on a strict financial diet once before and it had been a hell of a lot of hard work, but the psychological relief that came with having money in the bank and not living pay cheque to pay cheque had been worth every cent. I had learned a lot from Jason, including the art of self-control. It didn't mean I wasn't prone to a blow-out once every few weeks, but it no longer happened every week. Or every second day!

Other big changes were that I no longer smoked and I no longer had a car. But I was still a social creature through and through, and no amount of house-hunting, debt or work commitments was going to get rid of the fact that I did not like sitting at home on the couch every night watching TV. Never had, never would. I had also reinstated my $35 blow-wave most Friday lunchtimes. I had given up getting my hair done for almost 18 months when I was in hard-core savings mode, but since then I had decided I'd rather look and feel good than have bad hair, so had started my weekly ritual again.

There were also a few rather bad traits that had hung around from my dark, devious past. I still couldn't pay a bill on time and before I moved in with Julia and James I'd had to set up ongoing payment plans with every electricity, water, gas and phone company I was contractually obliged to dish money out to. And even when I borrowed my parents' or a friend's car, I still had an uncanny knack for getting parking fines and then ignoring them. I was just a little more prompt in paying than I had been in the past. At least now I could worry about fewer ongoing bills because utilities were included in my rent.

My relationship with parking inspectors had never been good, mainly because I was the type of girl who liked to park in the first available space regardless of the parking restrictions. I had received so many parking fines a few years earlier that I had been living in fear of debt collectors coming to my door. I did actually have almost every council in the city after me at one point before I had paid all the fines. When I got rid of my car I knew I wouldn't need to worry about racking up fines anymore, and it was just easier to walk, ride or catch public transport—on which I always bought a ticket!

By the time I saw Jason this time I had continued to boost my post–New York savings by putting away my usual $250 a week. I was proud of my savings efforts, but I knew he wanted me to be saving more. Yet I just couldn't seem to get there. Each week since moving house I had somehow needed to spend the extra $125 that I was supposed to be putting away for my deposit, so the surplus cash in my bank account every week was always spent. Somehow the extra cash went on going out, movies, books, music, magazines and clothes.

I sat down in Jason's office and proudly told him I had $35 500 in the bank. He didn't seem entirely impressed and handed over the new budget he had made for me.

Although I had kept up my savings plan and kept a vague budget in my head for the past 12 months, it had been a long time since I had absolutely stuck to a proper budget. It was a shock to see how regimented my life was going to become again. And even though I may have been acting as though saving each week was easy, it wasn't. I had a constant urge to spend cash on everything and anything that took my fancy.

The first familiar thing I saw on the new budget was the 'Pay yourself' row. Jason's 'Pay yourself first' concept was intended to help people save. Rather than keeping all your money in a single account where you would be more likely to spend it, he encouraged his clients to pay themselves the amount they wanted to save each week— into a separate account—as soon as they got paid their salary. I had two bank accounts: one for everyday usage and one for savings.

Jason talked me through the rest of the budget, saying he would prefer it if I could save some of the $141 left over each week, but I knew myself too well and realised I would need some leeway if I was going to successfully put $375 a week into a savings account and not touch it. There was over $7000 of difference in savings if I was able to do as Jason suggested, though.

Maggie Rose's budget
Maggie's income

	Weekly	Monthly	Annual
The City newspaper	$1154	$5000	$60 000
Freedom FM radio station	$96	$417	$5000
Less tax	($257)	($1113)	($13 350)
Total income	$993	$4304	$51 650

Maggie's expenses

	Weekly	Monthly	Annual
Savings — pay yourself	$375	$1625	$19 500
Rent	$150	$650	$7800
Health insurance	$20	$87	$1040
Contents insurance	$10	$43	$520
Telephone/mobile	$20	$87	$1040
Internet	$7	$30	$364
Public transport	$20	$87	$1040
Groceries	$100	$433	$5200
Eating out	$100	$433	$5200
Entertainment	$50	$217	$2600
TOTAL	**$852**	**$3692**	**$44 304**
Surplus	**$141**	**$612**	**$7346**

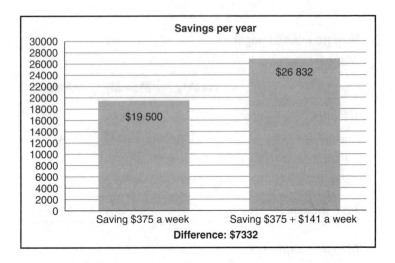

'This is going to take a massive amount of commitment from you, Maggie', Jason said. 'There is only a tiny proportion of the population who can actually be diligent enough to watch where every cent is being spent. Don't be too hard on yourself if you stuff up sometimes and break the budget. It just means it's going to take you a little longer to save your deposit.'

With the budget explained and out of the way, Jason then moved onto the cold, hard reality of buying property.

'As I said last time we met, buying a house is not just about having the deposit. When you purchase a house you need to cover a lot of extra costs before you can sign on the dotted line. These costs can really add up, Jason said in a serious tone I had not heard from him before. He sounded as though he should have had a snobby accent, and be wearing a robe and smoking a cigar. I wanted Livewire Jason back.

'On top of the price of the property, you are going to have to pay stamp duty, which is a percentage of the costs of the property; a transfer fee; a mortgage registration fee; a mortgage application fee; lender's mortgage insurance; and, finally, you will need to pay for a solicitor.'

My head was spinning; the only thing I'd heard of was the stamp duty, which is a state tax some people think is a rouse to bulk up the government's coffers. And thanks to Alex, I was well aware that I was going to need a property lawyer to draw up the legal documents to make the sale legit. Judging by how well things were going with us when Alex was actually in the country, I had figured he would happily do some pro bono work for me on that front.

'So how much would I need to get a $450 000 house, with all the added costs?'

'Close to $73 000, I'm afraid.'

I was shocked, but before I could respond, he pulled out a spreadsheet he had made, showing me how much it would actually cost me if I borrowed 90 per cent of the money I needed for a $450 000 home. The total of the funds needed—$72 897—was a reality check, to say the least.

'But keep in mind', Jason continued, 'that you'll also have the first home owner grant from the government. It's $7000 that the government will give you to put towards buying an established home and if you are planning to live in it rather than buy it as an investment. So in this case you could subtract $7000 from the funds that need to come from your own pocket.'

'What do you mean by "established home"?'

'An established home is a house that is already built. You would still get the grant if you were building a new home or moving to a regional area, but you may actually get more money in those cases. In your case you would be eligible for the $7000.'

COST ESTIMATE PURCHASE SCHEDULE

LENDER	—
Client's name	Maggie Rose
Property purchase price	$450 000
Stamp duty on property purchase	$18 970
Transfer registration fee	$1227
Mortgage registration	$100
Application fee	$600
Lender's mortgage insurance	$6000
Solicitor cost (your legal representative) estimated	$1000
Total costs	**$477 897**
Loan	**$405 000**
Lending value	**90%**
Funds to complete required	$72 897

Jason then talked me through the spreadsheet. Many of the expenses were self-explanatory; however, Jason had to explain to me that lender's mortgage insurance was insurance used by all lending institutions — banks, credit unions and building societies — to protect them if a person defaults on their home loan and can no longer afford the repayments, or if the person dies.

'And if a person is taking out a loan of 80 per cent or more of the cost of the house, the lender's insurance can be quite high because they see the home buyer as having a higher risk of defaulting. So basically, the more money you have saved, the less you are going to have dish out to the banks. That should be an incentive for you to really start putting some serious money away.

'I'm afraid I also need to warn you, Maggie, that with your current salary at $65 000, a bank may only be willing to lend you about $380 000. So even though we've just gone through the costs for a $450 000 house, you might need to be looking at place that costs closer to $400 000.'

I heard him loud and clear. It seemed that I might need to start looking at houses that were a hell of a lot cheaper than I had thought I could afford.

'Goodbye Leighton?' I said to Jason.

'I can't tell you where you need to buy, but what I have done is also made you out a cost estimate for a $340 000 loan on a purchase price of $400 000, just for your interest. Buying at that price and borrowing that amount means you would be lending 85 per cent of the purchase price — potential lenders would look upon this more favourably than 90 per cent. Of course, as you can see, you would need more money up-front if you only borrow 85 per cent of a $400 000 house. This is just a point of comparison for you, to show you that a lower lending value would mean you'd pay less mortgage insurance. I want you to have as much information as possible.'

After showing me the second spreadsheet, Jason continued with the not-so-good news.

'I do need to tell you', he began, 'that the cost analyses I showed you do not take into account the buffer.'

'The buffer?' I asked. 'What's that?' I was starting to feel overwhelmed by everything he was telling me.

Jason explained that if I was going to purchase a house I needed extra cash as a buffer for interest rate rises, renovations and anything else that came up.

COST ESTIMATE PURCHASE SCHEDULE

LENDER	—
Client's name	Maggie Rose
Property purchase price	$400 000
Stamp duty on property purchase	$17 476
Transfer registration fee	$1227
Mortgage registration	$100
Application fee	$600
Lender's mortgage insurance	$3824
Solicitor cost (your legal representative) estimated	$1000
Total costs	**$424 227**
Loan	**$340 000**
Lending value	**85%**
Funds to complete required	$84 227

'People constantly make the mistake of thinking that all they need is the deposit and the mortgage, and to have covered the immediate expenses. But what happens if you get sick or lose your job? What if interest rates go up four months in a row and you can't keep up with repayments?

'I have another chart for you to look at. This one shows you how much extra you would pay every time interest rates go up from a 7.79 per cent base.'

I sat and nodded my head, taking in the enormity of everything he was telling me.

Loan amount

Interest rate	Change	$150 000	$200 000	$250 000	$300 000	$350 000	$400 000	$450 000	$500 000
7.79%	0.00%	$0.00	$0.00	$0.00	$0.00	$0.00	$0.00	$0.00	$0.00
8.04%	0.25%	$24.77	$33.02	$41.28	$49.53	$57.79	$66.04	$74.30	$82.56
8.29%	0.50%	$49.75	$66.34	$82.92	$99.50	$116.09	$132.67	$149.26	$165.84
8.54%	0.75%	$74.95	$99.94	$124.92	$149.90	$174.89	$199.87	$224.85	$249.84
8.79%	1.00%	$100.36	$133.81	$167.27	$200.72	$234.17	$267.62	$301.08	$334.53
9.29%	1.50%	$151.78	$202.37	$252.97	$303.56	$354.15	$404.75	$455.34	$505.93
9.79%	2.00%	$203.97	$271.97	$339.96	$407.95	$475.94	$543.93	$611.92	$679.91
10.29%	2.50%	$256.90	$342.53	$428.17	$513.80	$599.43	$685.07	$770.70	$856.33
10.79%	3.00%	$310.52	$414.02	$517.53	$621.04	$724.54	$828.05	$931.55	$1035.06
11.29%	3.50%	$364.79	$486.39	$607.98	$729.58	$851.17	$972.77	$1094.37	$1215.96
11.79%	4.00%	$419.67	$559.57	$699.46	$839.35	$979.24	$1119.13	$1259.02	$1398.92
12.29%	4.50%	$475.14	$633.52	$791.90	$950.28	$1108.66	$1267.03	$1425.41	$1583.79
12.79%	5.00%	$531.14	$708.19	$885.24	$1062.29	$1239.33	$1416.38	$1593.43	$1770.48

'It's a really big deal—I can see that. I had no idea there were so many added costs. It seems criminal.'

'My advice to you, Maggie, is that you have at least an extra $5000 in your savings account when you find the house you want. That's $5000 on top of all the costs we've been discussing.

I thanked him for all his help, left his offices and started to have serious doubts about whether I was going to be able to pull off the purchase. And even if I managed to convince a bank to lend me any money, I was going to have to live out in the sticks at this rate.

The next day at work I changed the search settings on the real estate search site. Instead of looking only at Leighton with the option of showing results from surrounding suburbs, I changed the suburbs to definitely include Parklands and Monovale, as well as Clifton and Spright. Clifton and Spright were much further out than I had intended to go, but they were still reasonably nice suburbs and they were on a train line and, although they were too far out for me to walk to work, I could still walk to Leighton. I left the number of bedrooms as two, and the price range between $350000 and $450000. I knew Jason had said I was more likely to get a mortgage on a house that cost less than $400000, but I thought I would keep the upper end of my price range at $450000, just to see what was out there.

The results were more promising, even if I did still have my heart set on buying a place in Leighton. Within three days of broadening my search for a home, I had 10 houses to look at. Most were in Spright, but there was a nice cottage for sale in Clifton and another weatherboard place in Monovale to look at.

My confidence was growing and on the Thursday I filed my column an hour early so I could go to a couple of inspections to see exactly what I could afford in my price range.

The Clifton cottage's description sounded impressive. 'Funky open-plan living in an up-and-coming area', was the title on the website. The description continued, 'Two-bedroom home, with open-plan living and dining area. Small courtyard. ROW'. It sounded great and I thought there might have actually been a chance I could afford a reasonably nice place not too far out of the CBD. But when I turned up to the inspection it was a very different story. The terms 'cottage' and 'open-plan' were a slight overstatement.

I arrived just as the real estate agent was letting the first people in the door. The front of the house looked about three metres wide. There was a bedroom immediately to the left of the front door, which I assumed was the smaller of the two, but as I walked down the hall to the second room it was no more than two by two metres—possibly enough room for a study or a baby's room.

The open plan living/dining area was also tiny. In this case 'open-plan' simply meant no door in the wall between two rooms. Someone had literally cut a hole in the wall between the two rooms so the kitchen bench looked over a small lounge room. You then had to walk through the kitchen to get to the bathroom, which was bigger than the second bedroom and doubled as a laundry. As I walked, out the agent asked what I thought and I asked him what the asking price was.

'$380 000-plus.'

I choked.

The Monovale place, however, was impressive. It had been meticulously renovated and was exactly what I wanted: two spacious bedrooms, with a wide hallway leading into a big kitchen and living area. The owners had polished the floorboards, put in a new kitchen and bathroom, and given the whole house a fresh lick of paint. It even had a sweet courtyard with enough room for a table to sit outside with friends. It was a party house. I loved it. I left the place gushing and wishing I had enough money to put in an offer.

Rather than going home, I popped in to see my parents to give them a house-hunting update. When I first told them I planned to buy a house, they hadn't offered to lend me any money (and I hadn't asked!), so I took it as a sign they weren't in a position to do so, and I understood. I told Dad how incredible the Monovale house was and repeated the praises I had heaped on the real estate agent as I left. But instead of getting excited about the beautiful house with me, Dad launched into a lecture on the art of buying property.

'Never let the agent know you're interested, Maggie', Dad practically shouted at me across the table.

'Why not? I can't buy it, anyway.' I felt like I was 17 again was being lectured for something I'd done wrong.

'Maggie, you don't want the vendor to think there's too much interest in their house because they'll put the price up. You only need to talk to the agent if you are really interested and want to make an offer. Otherwise you're best just to say thanks and leave. They'll see you at the auction, anyway.'

I was sceptical, but when Mum came in and reiterated what Dad had said I was convinced. Mum had been the negotiator in all my parents' major purchases and she knew the art of getting the best deal.

'If you want us to come with you, we are always free, Maggie. It might be good for you to have someone who's bought a few houses to walk through and see if it's up to scratch.'

As I said, I loved my parents, but spending a weekend looking at houses with them was not my idea of a day off.

The weekend came and I went to watch the auction for the Clifton cottage on my own. I decided to have another walk through to see if it was really as bad as I'd thought it was. The master bedroom was as stifling and bland as I'd remembered. There was a faux fireplace in the corner that I hadn't seen on the first visit and it added absolutely nothing to the room. I could also see mould creeping down one of the walls, making the paint crackle and bubble.

As I turned to leave the room I heard a familiar voice. I just couldn't place it. Approaching the second, tiny bedroom I could see some people in the room already. I walked through the door and heard someone say my name.

'Maggie.'

It was Spencer and Angelica. This time I couldn't hide behind anyone. I cursed myself for not bringing Alex with me.

Once again, my heart lurched when I met Spencer's blue eyes. He smiled at me and for a brief second I forgot we'd ever broken up and smiled back. Then Angelica moved in for the kill and I could feel the smile wipe from my face.

'Maggie, how are you? It's so good to see you again. Isn't it, Spencer?' Angelica's act was so sickly sweet that I wanted to punch her.

'Hi, Angelica', I didn't know what else to say except, 'Good room for a baby.'

'That's just what I was saying to Spencer', Angelica said as she ruffled his thick black hair. They couldn't have been thinking about settling down! It was too soon. Surely they couldn't have been together for more than a year, because that would have meant Spencer moved on from me as soon as he got to Tokyo.

'Are you looking to buy?' Spencer asked.

'Obviously she is, honey. She wouldn't be here just to see you', Angelica butted in again, this time with a bemused tone.

'Yes, I'm looking to buy', I said shortly. 'I think the auction's about to start so it was nice to see you again. I'm going to head out onto the street. Good luck with the baby. Uh, I mean house-hunting.' Why did I have to bring up the baby?

As I bolted down the hallway I could hear what sounded like an argument between them. I pulled out my phone and quickly texted Eliza, Fran, Genevieve and Jem to tell them I had run into Spencer and Angelica again.

Once outside, I made a beeline for most crowded part of the street so Spencer and Angelica could not stand anywhere near me. I spied them exit the house and take up a position close to the auctioneer. I could see Spencer looking around the crowd anxiously. Was he looking for me?

The auctioneer started with the same hammy spiel as the agent at the last auction I'd been to. And while the agent at the house in Leighton had been suave, this guy had slicked back, greasy hair, was wearing a cheap suit and generally looked like the stereotypical dodgy real estate agent. However, he was doing an incredible job of making the pinhead-sized house sound spacious and luxurious.

'The vendor wants to sell today. This is a perfect opportunity for first home buyers to get into the real estate market and would be snapped up by renters if it was bought as an investment property', the auctioneer ranted.

The auction started and a man opened the bidding at $360 000. A woman then bid $370 000 and a third person came in at $385 000. It was already at the asking price. It was then that I started to feel someone's eyes upon me.

I turned my head and Spencer was staring at me. I was blushing and pretended I was engrossed in the auction before peering back to make sure I wasn't delirious.

Why was he looking at me? It was hard enough having to see him with another woman without him looking at me intently across a crowded street.

I could no longer hear what the auctioneer was saying, and when Angelica looked over at me, I jerked and put my hand up to my face to hide my red cheeks. My ears started ringing and my heart thumping. She kept staring at me with her big brown eyes. I started nodding my head to pretend I was agreeing with the auctioneer who was looking my way, saying something excitedly.

'$415 000. The house is on the market, so get in now if you want to be the winner. Going twice. This house is going to be sold today. Can I hear $1000?'

The crowd was quiet. I couldn't see who had made the last bid.

'The lady in black is going to take this property off the market', the auctioneer continued.

I couldn't see anyone in black. As I looked around, many people in the crowd turned and were staring at me. I looked down and saw that I was dressed in black.

'They must have confused me with the bidder', was all that crossed my mind.

But the auctioneer was gesturing towards me as well. I got the sickening feeling that I may have accidentally made the highest bid. I started to freak out.

Would they make me buy it? Would I be fined? What should I say? I wanted to die! Sweat started beading on my brow. I wanted to grab my phone and call someone for help. Who was going to get me out of this situation? Spencer certainly wasn't rushing to my aid.

The auctioneer's helper, another estate agent, suddenly sidled up to me in the crowd as all eyes darted around to see what would happen next. 'I like your style', he said to me quietly. 'I didn't even see that you were in the game. I reckon yours could be the knock-out bid to take this property off the market.'

I felt sick. 'I think there's been a mistake. Did I just bid on this house?' I stared at the man desperately.

'Well, you did bid and you nodded yes when I asked if you had indeed made the bid. So if no-one else bids after you then the house is yours. You did mean to bid, didn't you?'

'No, you see, I didn't mean to bid. I wasn't feeling well and I kind of went to a transient place for a moment.' My heart was racing and I had never been more freaked out in my entire life.

'So what you're telling me is that you didn't mean to bid? This is a very serious matter, miss. If no-one else bids and the house is sold, you're legally bound to purchase the property. Do you need to withdraw your bid?'

He suddenly turned and held up his hand to the auctioneer, signalling him to stop. Oh my goodness—this was going to be the most embarrassing moment I'd ever experienced. Maggie Rose halting an auction in front of a huge crowd of onlookers. In front of Angelica and Spencer!

But just at that very moment a young man in his 20s called out, '$417 000!'

I almost collapsed with relief, but no amount of apology was enough to placate the estate agent who'd been talking to me.

'Madam, I think you need to stay home next time you're not feeling well. This could have had very serious consequences—there are rules to auctions, you know. You shouldn't mess with this game.'

I watched as the auctioneer yelled 'sold' and called an end to the auction. The second estate agent turned from me and took the young man into the house. I didn't know what happened once you stepped inside the house with the auctioneer, but at that moment the thought of spending any one-on-one time with that particular real estate agent was terrifying.

By the time I had got my sullen, red face back on my bike I was no longer embarrassed about accidentally bidding on the house; it was the doing it in front of Spencer and Angelica part that was really irking me. They must have seen what happened and that I was completely flipping out, and they did nothing to help me out. And if they hadn't seen what had happened, then why didn't they come up to commiserate with me on missing out by only $1000?

They were probably in their cosy car laughing their heads off.

At dinner with Alex later that night, I gave him a blow-by-blow description of my cock-up—minus the part about Spencer and Angelica staring at me.

'Actually, while there are bidding terms within the contract of sale, you can't be forced to sign a contract and buy a property just because the auctioneer yelled out "sold"', Alex sounded like a seriously intelligent lawyer, and I felt even more stupid. 'But why exactly did he think you bid?'

'I just spaced out and must have looked like I was bidding. I think I scratched my nose or touched my eye or something.'

He suddenly burst into fits of laughter, and I joined him. He looked at me fondly. I knew he was laughing with me, not at me.

Alex and I had been seeing each other for nearly five months — minus the two-and-a-half that he had been overseas during that time. I liked that he wasn't serious most of the time, and that he was relaxed. He also gave me back some of the confidence that had gone missing in the previous 12 months. He always tried to make me feel special and I thought it was especially sweet when he turned his phone off so he could concentrate on me. He was going back to Europe in a fortnight's time and I wanted to test the waters to see how keen he actually was. I needed to get seeing Spencer out of my mind, anyway.

'So, do you think I'll be getting a few extra phone calls when you're away this time?'

'I'm sorry I haven't been great at calling while I've been travelling. I'm just really busy and prefer to use email rather than sounding too rushed to talk.'

'You'll be away for a month again. I know you're busy but surely I warrant a few calls.'

'I promise to be a more diligent lover.'

So that's what I was. A lover. I'd never been anyone's lover in my life. It was a little bit thrilling.

'Why don't you just take me with you?' I asked brazenly, feeling a rush of seductiveness.

'That's not a good idea at the moment, unfortunately. But one day', Alex said, shutting me down. 'If I were to take you, you would be on your own for 90 per cent of the trip. When I'm away for work, I'm flat out. And you have focus on finding your dream home. And when you do, I'll happily do the property conveyancing for you.'

A seed of doubt about him was planted in my mind as I felt I had been given the brush-off. But the doubt quickly died when he leaned over to kiss me. I was certain he was dead keen on me. Why would he have wanted to spend so much time with me if he wasn't? He was a 36-year-old man and definitely not into mucking around. He was also the one who had pursued me. Still, he could have humoured me a little about travelling with him.

The next week at work was flat out and I was so busy I forgot to worry about seeing Angelica at the radio station on the Thursday morning. I arrived at my usual time and read over the notes I'd made. The radio show's host, Darren, was pretty laid back, but sometimes there were last-minute changes to the program and Angelica briefed me on them before going to air. I hadn't seen Angelica that morning at all, so assumed it was business as usual. When I sat down in the studio this time, Darren had a strange look on his face, as though he was about to start laughing but was controlling himself.

'Okay listeners, I'm here with our regular Thursday guest reporter, Maggie Rose. But instead of talking shop, we are going to talk real estate', he looked directly at me. 'Maggie, a little birdie told us you were bidding at an auction last Saturday. And you had an interesting bidding style. Can you tell us a bit about your strategy?'

'No, Darren, there was a mix-up. I didn't actually mean to bid', I said. While trying to think of a way to get him off the topic as quickly as possible I had, of course, inadvertently dumped myself in it—why didn't I just play along and pretend that I had meant to make the bid?

'Well, my lovely producer Angelica told me it was quite something to see, and that you were really psyching out the other bidders! Isn't that right Angelica?' He looked past me through the glass wall of the studio.

I spun my chair around and saw Angelica standing there at her computer, smirking at me while nodding at Darren. I gave her a look of disgust. She knew that I had made an embarrassing mistake, and now she just wanted me to squirm and try talk my way out of it!

So, rather than falling into her trap, I decided to relay the whole story blow-by-blow…with a couple of white lies thrown in for good measure. Darren was captivated as I told him about running into an old flame in a shoebox-sized room of a house about to be auctioned. I went on to say that the ex had, for some strange reason, kept staring at me for the duration of the auction. I made no mention of blushing and hiding away; I said the reason the auctioneer thought I had bid was because I was trying to tell the ex to stop giving me googly eyes while his girlfriend was standing right next to him.

The part I didn't change was the conversation with the estate agent at the end of the auction. And that was what really cracked Darren up. He wanted to know all about my other real estate misadventures and said from that day on he expected a little update each week so that listeners could keep up to date with my quest to find a home.

Out of the corner of my eye I could see Angelica fuming, but I didn't care anymore. I was not going to be pushed around by a skinny girl who was going out with my ex-boyfriend. She could have him, as far as I was concerned. When I left the studio she was standing in her booth staring straight ahead and I knew I had really pissed her off.

'Job done', I proudly told myself.

When I arrived at work 30 minutes later, everyone in the office who had listened came over to congratulate me on getting out of such a difficult situation with flare. Genevieve told me everyone knew who I was talking about because Janice had made a big song and dance about how rude I was being, talking about Spencer like that. Spencer had been a popular person when he worked at *The City*, but I was the underdog in the situation and I could tell people were glad I didn't fall apart on air.

After feeling so strange about Spencer being back, I was vindicated. He was going out with a complete brat. I was not going to let either one of them worry me again.

My dad had begged to come with me to some inspections and auctions, so on my third Saturday of serious house-hunting I let him chauffer me around for the day. It was a good day to be driven around—it was raining and I was hung-over from having been out the night before.

My revelations about not letting Angelica and Spencer worry me also meant that I felt prepared to run into them again. I was a little concerned about Dad seeing Spencer, though. He'd seen how upset I was when we broke up, and I didn't want there to be any sort of confrontation, especially if Dad saw Spencer with another woman. Despite my own confidence, I hoped we didn't see them.

Dad picked me up at 8.30 am for breakfast and an hour of looking at the paper before the first inspection at 10 am in Monovale. He had a full day planned, and it was going to be a whirlwind tour of the city's open for inspections, with a couple of auctions thrown in for good measure. I could tell Dad was excited to be able to help me. I was pretty sure my brothers never asked him or Mum for help when they bought their homes, so I was letting him be a father for a moment.

The Monovale house had looked good in the advertisement.

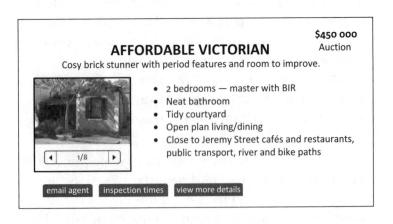

AFFORDABLE VICTORIAN

$450 000
Auction

Cosy brick stunner with period features and room to improve.

- 2 bedrooms — master with BIR
- Neat bathroom
- Tidy courtyard
- Open plan living/dining
- Close to Jeremy Street cafés and restaurants, public transport, river and bike paths

1/8

email agent   inspection times   view more details

Again, the agent had failed to say that the property was only big enough to house a family of midgets. The pictures online had looked great. It was nice and clean and didn't need a whole lot of things changed to make a more elegant abode. However, the vendor was asking for $450 000 and at every single auction I'd been to the house had gone for at least $40 000 more than the advertised price. I assumed this place would be no different when it was auctioned.

Feeling dejected, we drove on to another place in Monovale that had been advertised within my price range. It was slightly more promising. The master bedroom was huge and the second bedroom was also a reasonable size. It was also the first place I had inspected that did not have an open-plan living/dining area. Instead, there was an airy kitchen, with a separate living room.

As we were leaving I spotted Spencer getting out of a car down the road. Before Dad had a chance to get a brochure from the agent, I had grabbed his arm and raced him to the car to avoid any more unnecessary confrontations. Dad had no idea what was going on and had started the car and sped off before realising the oddness of what was happening and asked for an explanation.

'I just saw someone I really didn't want to talk to.'

'Who?'

I had to come up with a quick lie. My parents had loved Spencer and had been extremely angry with him for breaking my heart. I didn't want to bring the whole thing up again and see my dad get upset.

'Someone I interviewed for a story at work. I didn't go well and he'd left abusive messages on my phone after the story was published.'

We must have gone to eight inspections in four hours and were finishing the day with two auctions, both in Spright. The first auction went as expected; the house sold for $60000 more than it was advertised.

What were these bloody real estate agents doing? I could not understand why they couldn't just advertise the houses for what they were actually worth. I knew house prices were inflated, but it seemed the real estate industry had a tiny blind spot when it came to telling it as it was.

Extremely frustrated, I wanted to go home after the first Spright auction. Dad convinced me to see the last place and as I needed to go to the bathroom I said yes. My plan was to try to sneak into the bathroom at the auction house — though I had no idea if this was actually allowed! The rain was bucketing down when we pulled up to the house. I bolted to the front door and ran into the agent from the auction where I had accidentally bid. It had been two weeks and I was pretty sure he would have forgotten me by that time.

'Hi. Just wanting to have a quick look around before you get started', I said, smiling sweetly. He was terrifying.

'Madam, nice to see you again. The auction will be starting in a few moments.'

Grr, he recognised me.

Everyone was filtering out of the house as dad and I went running around poking into rooms. There was a water feature in the backyard and with the sound of tinkling water I could suddenly think of nothing other than the fact that I really needed to pee. As we neared the front door, I left Dad with the umbrella to go back out onto the street, and doubled back to use the toilet before the auction began. The house was empty as I snuck down the hallway, snuck into the bathroom and locked the door. Thinking I had got away with using a complete stranger's bathroom, I relaxed, but it was less than 10 seconds before I heard footsteps coming down the hallway and then there was a knock at the door.

The agent! Damn.

'Is there someone in there?'

But it wasn't the agent. I knew that voice anywhere — it was Spencer. I didn't answer. Instead I sat frozen to the loo while Spencer jiggled the door handle attempting to get in.

He seemed to give up. I quickly got up, made myself nice and stood by the door listening for signs that he was still hanging around. No noise. Phew—I'd gotten away with it.

But when I opened the door to leave and looked down the hallway Spencer was standing there with the agent. They both spun around at the sound of the door opening.

'Maggie, what are you doing?' Spencer asked.

'Yes, madam, what are you doing? It is not acceptable to use the bathroom at an auction', the smarmy agent said.

'I'm sorry. If it's any consolation, I didn't go through the medicine cabinet', I said, speaking without thinking once again. The agent cleared his throat loudly, sending shivers down my spine.

'Can I just have a moment?' I gasped, lunging back inside the bathroom. I looked in the bathroom mirror to see that my entire face and neck had come out in a blotchy scarlet hue. 'Oh, Maggie Rose', I said to myself. 'Why do you do these things?'

It took all my courage to walk back down the hallway, squeeze past the auctioneer, who was clearly waiting to start the auction, and outside to find my dad. By that stage the crowd was five-deep and huddled under the trees outside the house in an attempt to stay dry. I found my dad standing to the side of the turnout, with Spencer.

Why was this happening to me?

'Maggie, look who I ran into.' My dad sounded really happy to see him. Angelica wasn't anywhere to be seen.

'Hi, Spencer, what a surprise to see you here', I said, ignoring the fact that he had just caught me using the toilet.

Spencer walked over and kissed me on the cheek. My cheeks were burning.

'How are you? I've been meaning to get in touch and see how you're going', he said, as though what had happened between us was merely water under the bridge.

'Thanks, I'm really good. Work's going well. Not much more to tell you, really', I answered, staccato, like a robot.

And it was true that I was good. I didn't want to launch into the full details of my life with him, though. 'Where's Angelica?' I asked, changing the subject and hoping, if I'm honest, to make him uncomfortable.

'She couldn't make it today and asked me to come along instead.'

I know I was flummoxed, but it sounded as if he was seeing the house for her. That could mean they weren't buying a place together after all. But it didn't seem logical for him to look at houses for her if he wasn't going to be moving in with her! All I could conclude was that they must be planning for her to buy and him to move in. Still shacking up. Still devastating.

I didn't want to have to see him anymore. I wanted to move on, and our little weekend rendezvous were making me feel like crap, regardless of my resolution that I would forget about him.

'That's nice. And how's your work going?' I said hiding my contempt for having to talk to him.

Before he could answer, Dad broke in.

'Spencer's just been telling me about his new job at the Metro network as the nightly news director. Pretty impressive.'

'Congrats', I said trying to sound sincere.

'Maggie seems to be doing well, too', he was addressing my father. 'She's great on the radio, especially since she talked about her auction experiences. She's got a real gift.' He turned to me with a twinkle in his eye. 'I always knew you'd do really well.'

I had no idea what he was trying to do. He was flirting with me, or at least being really, really nice. It wasn't that I thought he was going to be a nasty prick or anything; I mean, Spencer was always a genuinely lovely person. Even when he told me he was going to Tokyo and said he decided on behalf of both of us that I shouldn't go with him, there had been a fleeting moment when I had felt like the bad guy in the situation. It hadn't lasted, though.

But why on earth was he bringing up my job when it was the sole reason he had said I couldn't go with him to Japan?

I tried to concentrate on the auction, but I didn't want to move away from Spencer, as that would have made it obvious that I was uncomfortable. The auction started with the auctioneer making a quip clearly aimed at me.

'Anyone here today with no intention of bidding, please make sure you are in a sound state of mind and that you keep your hands in your pockets.'

I could see Spencer smirking, while Dad stood there clueless to what was going on.

As predicted, the house went for way more than the asking price. On the way home, Dad chatted away about how nice it had been to see Spencer again, and I wanted to jump out of the moving car and run home to my bed.

***

I decided I needed a few weeks off from the property game for my own peace of mind. It wasn't only the act of running into Spencer every Saturday that was doing my head in (despite what I tried to tell myself!), it was the fact that I really thought I liked Alex, and seeing Spencer was confusing me. I guess the fact that Alex didn't seem overtly keen for a serious relationship made it easier for my mind to wander. But seeing Spencer was making me feel miserable.

I had also begun to realise just how far away I was from owning my own home. In the previous three years the city's property prices had soared to become the most expensive in the country. Prices had increased about 10 to 15 per cent per year for the past three years, and I feared I would be saving forever before I could actually get a mortgage. From what I could gather from news reports, the inflation in costs was a first, and everyone seemed to have an opinion on whether it was going to continue to boom, whether it would bust or whether it would plain old slow down. I wanted the bust.

Interest rates were also tipped to rise, which meant I would need to have more in the bank before I could consider applying for a loan.

My savings were coming along, but I was a little behind schedule. As Jason had said, it was really hard to save $375 a week on my salary, let alone the extra $141 on top of that. It was already June and I should have had a few thousand more than the $37 000 I had in the bank.

I settled back into work and stopped obsessing about finding the perfect home and getting my deposit together. I decided life was too short to stress myself out. I stopped jumping on the computer every five minutes to see if any new places had gone up for sale and limited myself to looking once a day. I even stopped worrying about seeing Angelica at the radio station. Although I wasn't sure what I was going to say to Darren when he heard I was on a house-hunting hiatus for a few weeks.

For the three weeks I had been talking house with Darren, my segment had become a mini hit. The first 15 minutes of the 20-minute segment were still taken up by my wrap of the news for the day and the last five were dedicated to talking real estate. As it was only a short amount of time to talk about the weekend's hunting, I had stuck to the basics — that is, how every house I went to see was advertised below what the vendor actually wanted, running into the mean real estate agent again and, of course, the etiquette of using a bathroom at an auction or open for inspection.

Some good news also finally came my way. I was offered a guest spot on a yet-to-be-launched news talk panel for 18 to 39 year olds called *The Real Nightly News*. A woman called Isobel from Metro TV contacted me and said my name had been put forward as a potential guest. She said my editor had already given me the green light and I needed to come in and have a screen test the next week.

Things were actually starting to move along in my career. I had no idea why, though. To say I was shocked to be asked to go on TV was a gross understatement; I was speechless. I didn't have to wonder for too long to work out who had put my name forward — it had to be my editor; she was always trying to find ways to promote *The City* brand and a TV show was the perfect vehicle. It was an offer too good to refuse, even if it did mean I would have to reveal myself to the world with an extra four kilograms of TV weight added to my already generous proportions, and even if there was a slim chance of running into Spencer while at the studio, as he worked at Metro. I said yes on the spot, and told Isobel I'd see her the next Monday for the screen test.

But good news at work wasn't enough. I needed to take my mind off the house-hunting and Spencer business, and I knew exactly what would do the trick.

When I lived alone, my greatest pleasure was hosting dinner parties on a budget. I had a knack for making people think I'd spent a lot of money while remaining frugal. Of course there were times when I would splash out, but if I wanted to cook and see my friends without spending a whole load of cash, I was actually capable of keeping it together.

Because I was sharing a house, it had become impossible for me to have anyone over for dinner unless they were willing to sit at a table for two. I had offered to bring my larger table to the house when I moved in, but James and Julia were attached to their tiny table. The second problem was that my housemates were always home. They were a nice couple; I just didn't want to socialise with them. And when anyone had popped in to say hi, I had taken to escorting him or her to my bedroom to drink tea on the bed. Not an ideal situation and definitely not a way to make a good impression.

With my house out of the equation, I called upon Max to let me host a dinner at his and Jem's house with its almost-finished renovations. Apart from one afternoon when Jem had come to see my new pad, when she had been forced to sit on the windowsill in my room because my housemates were watching a DVD in the open-plan living area, I had barely seen them in months. They had been renovating their home flat-out and I had not been socialising.

I rang Jem and offered to cook if they would allow me to use their house for the dinner. Being too nice to say no, Jem humoured me and obliged. I had a feeling their kitchen was going to be spectacular and it had been months since I had cooked for more than one person — quite depressing in the scheme of things. Alex was also back from his trip and I had decided it was time for him to meet my friends. If Eliza had not known him from university I'm pretty sure they would have all thought I had invented him to make myself feel better.

Whenever I was getting ready for a dinner party at my old place I would do all my shopping at Gerry's. Gerry's was a gourmet supermarket in Leighton that had every deluxe ingredient under the sun. It was rather pricey, but I had found a new recipe that allowed me to use beautiful ingredients while remaining astute with my savings.

There were going to be eight people at the dinner: Max, Jem, Fran and her new man, Patrick — a guy she met on our night out at the club, not the hot date she'd previously told us about — Tim, Yvette, Alex and myself. Since my financial trouble a few years back, I was well practised in cooking on the cheap and I worked out that I wanted to spend around $10 per person for the meal, which still allowed me to get the really special ingredients from Gerry's. Tim, who was a cook, said he'd do dessert; Max said he'd sort out the wine and Fran offered to bring a starter. Dinner was sorted.

I hadn't had a chance to see Alex since he had arrived back in the country, so he volunteered to drive me around town to get the food and so we could catch up. It was good to see him again. There was a lot to talk about on my end, and I ranted about the TV job, house-hunting and getting caught in the loo at the auction. Alex didn't seem so keen to shed any light on his trip, saying it was 'Same old, same old'. The only thing he was willing to reveal was that he had spent most of his time in London and Paris and said he wanted to take me there someday. I should have melted, but his unwillingness to talk about travelling unnerved me. If he was so keen on me, why wasn't he more open to developing our relationship? Was he hiding something from me? Maybe he had another lover. I wasn't prepared to ask him, though.

I was cooking tuna and lemon risotto. Apart from being delicious, it was also dirt cheap to make and fitted my proposed budget per head—at least, that was until I got to Gerry's with Alex. He was much more enthusiastic about dinner parties than he was about talking work.

While I shopped for the essential ingredients, Alex was off choosing cheese, champagne, olives and wine. I tried to tell him other people were providing all of these things, but he was insistent. He was like a kid in a candy store. I waited for him with my groceries and walked over to the cashier. He signalled for me to put my things on the conveyor with his. The cashier started scanning the champagne and cheese, and the numbers started flying. The total grocery bill came out to $300. Oh, no.

I gasped as I reached for my EFTPOS card—my $10 per head budget was completely blown! And I didn't want seem stingy by asking Alex to pay for the extra things he'd selected.

I was so relieved when Alex held up his hand and said, 'No, it's on me, Maggie Rose. We haven't seen each other in weeks and I really want to make it up to you'.

Despite my relief I did miss being able to spend money on nice things, and I felt like a complete cheapskate!

The night went on to be one of those magical events when everything goes right. My friends loved Alex and for the first time in months I stopped thinking about house-hunting and Spencer. We stayed up until 4 am drinking, talking and dancing before Alex took me back to his apartment where I stayed until I had to get up to go to the TV screen test on the Monday morning.

Having never been on television, I had no idea what I was in for with the test screening. Thinking they were going to throw me in the deep end, I got up a few hours earlier than usual, left Alex in bed and headed back to my place to get ready. I blearily put on a full face of make-up and did my best attempt at a blow wave, trying my hardest to look TV-ready.

The Metro TV studios were in Monovale, and after what felt like about 25 minutes of security checks I was allowed to go through to reception and ask for Isobel. When she came out of the lift I was gobsmacked. Isobel was breathtakingly beautiful without a single skerrick of make up on her perfect face. In comparison, I must have looked like a blond Marilyn Manson with my full face of makeup including smoky eyes.

Feeling a little intimidated, I silently followed Isobel along the corridor to her office. It seemed strange to be walking the corridor of a big TV network; I'd never dreamed that anyone would want me to be on television. We sat down and she made me some coffee. I was ready to be grilled on my knowledge of current affairs, but instead Isobel started chatting about her weekend and asking how mine went. When we eventually got around to talking about what I was there for, I was pleasantly surprised to hear the idea behind the program I had been chosen for.

'Let me talk you through what we are proposing', Isobel began. '*The Real Nightly News* is going to be a weekly talk show discussing the big issues of the week but with a young, political and comedic slant. Think Jon Stewart with a panel.'

'It sounds great, I'm just not sure what I can offer', I replied. 'I'm not in any way remotely famous and I don't have a knack for comedy... as far as I know, anyway!'

Isobel laughed and said I wouldn't need to worry as I was suggested because I was young and a fresh talent— what she meant was that no-one knew who I was, and I was under 40!

Isobel and I talked for an hour like we were old friends before she stood up and led me down the hall for my screen test.

'You just need to go in there and have your hair and make-up done before we get started', Isobel said, pointing to a door.

'I already have make-up on.'

'Yes, I know', she smiled knowingly. 'But no-one does their own make up in TV. How else do you think everyone hides the four kilograms you gain from the camera? Don't worry, you are in great hands with Madeleine. She is lovely and happens be the best in the business.'

I was ushered into a chair and introduced to Madeleine, the hair and make-up artist. Isobel was right; Madeleine was an expert. She washed my hair and blow-waved it perfectly, then did my make up with an actual air brush. I had never had my make-up professionally done in my life. It was amazing and I never wanted to go back to my old face again!

The screen test consisted of me sitting in front of a camera and talking to Isobel. It was all over in 10 minutes. Isobel told me I would only be needed once a fortnight if they decided to use me, but she said she was sure the executive producer would want me. I, on the other hand, was sure they weren't going to call me. But having great hair and make-up at 10 on a Monday morning was enough to put a pep in my step.

***

Two weeks later I hadn't heard a thing from Metro, but I received some other good news. Grace, my friend in New York, had had a healthy baby boy. She sent me a barrage of photos and it was enough to make me want to jump on a plane and go back and visit them. But even though I'd toned down the house-hunt, I still wanted to save my money—I knew I wanted to buy a house eventually.

I had spent almost every night with Alex and the only house-hunting I had done was from my computer. I had been avoiding inspections because I hadn't come across a single house that was worth going to see.

It was late June and I had saved $37 500. I clearly hadn't been keeping exactly to Jason's budget, as my savings had only increased by $500 in four weeks. I just wasn't that interested anymore, and I even started considering moving back into a place on my own again.

That's when I saw The One. It was on the outskirts of Parklands; it seemed perfect for a first home buyer and affordable to boot.

I had a really good feeling about this place. Sure, I'd read ads for lots of places that seemed great on paper, and in real life they were terrible, but somehow this place was different. I don't know how, exactly, but the photos inspired me. The floorplan looked perfect. At the very least, it was enough to pique my interest and get me back in the game. I *had* to see this house. And I also needed to concentrate on getting that damn deposit.

Lessons learned

- You won't save much money if you don't stick to your budget!
- There are a lot more costs associated with buying a house and getting a mortgage than you might expect— any bank or mortgage broking website will have a breakdown of the types of costs to expect.
- Never wear full-on make-up at 8 am in the morning. It doesn't look good—especially not next to a TV glamazon.
- Winning at an auction isn't a legally binding agreement— nothing is sold until you put your signature on the contract.
- Don't lose hope when house-hunting— you will need to sift through a lot of rot before you find a gem.
- It is not okay to use the toilet when at an inspection or an auction.

PART III

The emotional purchase: we've all been there

July to September

Dream home: found in Parklands; perfectly presented two-bedroom cottage with a rustic garden; just 9 km from the CBD; train line on the doorstep

Savings: $37500

Deposit needed: not really sure anymore

Happiness: elated

The first chance I had to inspect the Parklands house was a week later and, amazingly, it was just as beautiful as it had been described on the website. Unlike every other house I had inspected, number 3 Treasury Street was even better in the flesh than the website made it out to be; something of a revelation in my time looking for a home.

The high ceilings gave the living area an ethereal feeling. The two bedrooms were huge and had brand-spanking-new floor-to-ceiling built-in wardrobes. The bathroom was about a decade old, but had fabulous black-and-white chequered tiles and a huge shower big enough for two, while the kitchen had new bench tops and appliances. However, the pièce de résistance was the paved courtyard, which had ivy- and lavender-drenched brickwork on the ground and walls and built-in benches. The owner had set up a rustic table and chairs and had also perfectly scattered cushions over the benches. It was like stepping into a courtyard in Tuscany. I decided that when I bought it I would fit out the courtyard exactly as the owner had.

I had never felt such a tangible, burning desire to own something in my entire life. Although I had never been great with money, I was never a shopaholic. But I suddenly felt extreme empathy for any woman who had longed for an uber-expensive handbag or had been sent mad over the latest pair of $2000 Jimmy Choos. The Property Gods had finally blessed me and I was willing to sacrifice anything to make this house mine.

Like a woman possessed, I inspected the house three times in two weeks; leaving the agent in no doubt that I was interested. Playing it cool I was not. I would also dreamily look through the online photos of the house and imagine myself living there. I could see a life for myself in the small, but lovely, living area. I could see my bed fitting beautifully into the master bedroom. The rest of my furniture and the new items I imagined buying would suit the house perfectly. And I was sure Alex would love it, too. I could see my friends sitting in the courtyard laughing and talking, while I played the dutiful hostess at my beautiful home.

Although I had no idea whether I could really afford this place, I was so devoted to buying it that I even managed to put away half my wage each week and added an extra $800 to my savings to take my deposit to $38 300 within a fortnight.

The only reasons I could come up with for the owner asking for only a minimum of $400 000 as a private sale were that it was on a very small block and it happened to back onto a train line. The proximity to the railway tracks didn't deter me in the slightest from wanting the house. I had lived in London in a place where there was non-stop noise, and for my own little piece of heaven I was willing to put up with practically anything.

From my (albeit limited) experience, I was sure the house would have gone for closer to $550 000, at the very least, if it had been auctioned. Max and Jem came and saw it with me and agreed.

'It's stunning, Maggie. You have to put in an offer. I'm pretty sure this house, at this price, only comes around once in a lifetime', Jem said when we all went to have a coffee after we had inspected the place.

'I want to, but I'm not sure I can get a mortgage yet, or how much I'd be able to get. And I don't know the first thing about private sales.'

'Just go for it', Max added. 'I'm pretty sure you just have to put in an offer to the agent. And of course you'll be able to get a loan.'

'You must be close to having your deposit together by now', broke in Jem. 'If this is your dream home and if it is meant to be, everything will fall into place.'

'Just like it did for Jem and me.' Max and Jem were tag-teaming in their excitement.

I desperately wanted to believe what they were saying. To fall in love with something so quickly had to be fate. But how could I just call a bank and get a mortgage? The thought of getting my hands on that much money so easily was unfathomable.

I also knew very little about the actualities of getting a home loan and, because of that, the thought of buying Treasury Street should have been banished from my mind. It's just that it was the perfect house and I knew that if I missed out I would spend the rest of my life going out of my way to walk past this house and look longingly at the front door, wishing it were mine.

My obsession with the house saw my attention span all but collapse. When I was supposed to be writing, I was either looking at the house online or looking for furniture that would complement the period features and the furniture I already owned. I was acting more like a woman who had met the man of her dreams and had started planning her wedding, not someone who had simply seen a house that she probably couldn't afford.

One Monday morning three weeks after initially finding the house and two days after my fifth visit, I decided I was going to put in an offer. In the midst of one of my daydreams I started researching private sales on the government's consumer affairs website. I read that a person could put in an offer on a house being sold in a private sale and it could be 'conditional' of just about anything you can think of, which the vendor would accept. This meant I could put in an offer without having the money right there and then. Bingo! The website said I had at least three days to change my mind about buying the house and/or get the finance for it. All I had to do was put in my offer along with a minimum $500 deposit that was refundable if my offer was 'gazumped', or outbid, by someone else.

As a journalist, the majority of my days were spent researching, so I started scouring the web for different types of home loans. The large banks had a home loan 'preliminary pre-approval' function where customers could insert a few of their financial details and find out how much money they could borrow.

When I saw the term 'pre-approval', I initially thought getting pre-approval would give me carte blanche to walk into the real estate agent selling Treasury Street and walk out with the keys. Just like that. But the first thing I found out was that applying for preliminary pre-approval on a website does not mean the bank has actually committed to lending you the money. The reality is that, in most cases, preliminary pre-approval is so preliminary that all it means is that after applying for the pre-approval the bank will call you to discuss actually lending you the money. Preliminary pre-approval is like an 'expression of interest' in the home loan.

Nevertheless, I decided to put my financial details into the websites of five banks for preliminary pre-approval. The first bank wanted specific information about what type of loan I wanted to apply for, my marital status, if I had a deposit (and how much), what my income was and what my major expenses were. It was here that I ran into trouble — I had no idea what the different types of loans were. Clearly I had to do some more research.

The various websites of banks and non-bank lenders had web pages dedicated to first home buyers who, like me, didn't know a lot about what they were doing and, like me, needed to be taught 'Getting a Mortgage 101'. The Universal Bank seemed to have the most comprehensive explanation of the different types of loans, but I still felt that I needed to talk to someone in person so they could explain all the terms that I didn't understand. So, what would I normally do when researching a story and I wanted to find out more information? I would interview someone appropriate.

My column was in good shape, so I snuck away from work at lunchtime and went to my local Universal Bank branch. I walked through the sliding doors and onto the very bank-ish royal blue carpet. It was lunchtime and the bank was in the midst of its midday rush. I went to the information counter and asked the staff member if I could see a home loan adviser to talk about the different types of loans they offered. She said the bank would be happy to help and told me to take a number. Someone would be with me shortly.

I sat on a chaise with the three other people who were waiting, and suddenly I became nervous. What if the loan adviser thought I wanted to take out a home loan here and now! I wondered if I was actually allowed to just enquire.

But when the next available adviser called my number, she was very helpful and I took notes as I would for a regular interview.

'Are you wanting to apply for a loan today?' she asked first.

'No. I just want to get an idea of the different types of loans you have and what information you need from me if I want to apply.'

'Right. There are four main criteria you will have to pass for the bank to lend you the money for a home loan', she began. 'The first thing we would want to know is how much you have saved. Then we will want to know how much money you want to lend and what your capacity is to pay back the loan.'

'What do you mean by "capacity"?'

'Your capacity is your ability to pay back the debt. It's called the "debt-to-income ratio". For example, if your home loan is going to cost you about $2400 per month and your monthly income is $4800, then your debt-to-income ratio is 50 per cent. Fifty per cent is as low as the bank will go for a debt-to-income ratio in most cases, by the way.'

I was furiously writing everything down while trying to do the sums in my head at the same time. Maybe it would have made more sense to just apply for a loan and get it over and done with.

'The next criterion is your credit history', she continued. 'We want to see a good track record of savings and we will also do a credit check. This is the biggest hurdle for some people. Your history must be impeccable for you to be approved for a loan.'

As soon as the words 'credit check' came out of her mouth, my own mouth went dry. Throughout my 20s, credit was my best friend, and I'd taken a long time to pay back several of my debts. Although I was pretty sure I had no ongoing or outstanding debts, I wondered whether I would actually pass a credit check because of my history. I lost all my confidence again, but the loan adviser continued talking, so I didn't have time for a crisis. I'd worry about the credit check later.

'The final piece of information we will need before we give you a mortgage is a valuation on the house. We will get an independent valuer to go out and assess the property to make sure the house is worth what you have bought it for.'

'You mean the price I'd offered to pay for the house wouldn't suffice as its value?' I asked.

'No. We need to make sure the amount we lend is the right amount. Because if you, for some reason or another, can no longer pay the loan and the house has to be sold, the bank needs to make sure it will get its money back.'

That made sense.

The home loan specialist again asked me if I wanted to sign up for a loan and, again, I said no. I told myself I was in research mode and wasn't ready for an actual loan yet, despite my dream home already being on the market. Instead, I asked her to explain the different types of home loans the bank offered.

Back at work, I typed up the notes I'd taken on the three most popular types of home loans the loan adviser had mentioned, to get them clear in my mind. I should have been concentrating on my column, but I just couldn't think about anything but owning Treasury Street.

Variable home loan — principal and interest repayments

A home loan that increases and decreases in accordance with the Reserve Bank's interest rate movements. If the Reserve Bank puts interest rates up, the home loan repayments will increase; if rates go down, so will the loan repayments.

Pros

Repayments would be less if interest rates fell

Often offered at a lower introductory rate than other home loans

Cons

Repayments would be more if interest rates rose

Fixed rate home loan — principal and interest repayments

The interest rate on the loan will be fixed for a fixed term — between one and five years. So, the interest rate stays the same regardless of whether the Reserve Bank raises or lowers its rates. Once the fixed term period is complete, you can change the type of loan. It is still a long-term loan (usually 25–30 years); it just means that when your fixed period has expired you can choose a type of loan that is right for you.

Pros

Offers security for the fixed term — you are not vulnerable to having to pay larger amounts when interest rates increase during that period

Cons

If interest rates decrease, you do not reap the benefits of paying less on the mortgage each month

Split rate home loan — Principal and interest repayments

Part of the loan is fixed and part of the loan is variable, and you can choose how much is allocated to each part.

Pros

The entire amount required as a repayment does not increase if interest rates rise

Better than a variable loan for budgeting purposes because a specific proportion of the mortgage repayments are locked in at a fixed rate

Cons

If interest rates decrease, you do not reap the benefits of paying less on the entire amount of the mortgage each month

The adviser at Universal also told me that the three loans we'd discussed required that the mortgagee (the borrower) immediately start repaying both the principal amount and the interest on the loan; this was known as a principal + interest loan. She explained to me that the 'principal' amount is the amount actually borrowed, whereas the 'interest' is the rate of interest the lender charges the borrower on the amount they have borrowed. Taking out a principal + interest loan would mean I'd have to immediately start repaying the amount I had borrowed for the house, plus the interest on that amount.

Some loans actually allow the mortgagee to choose whether they want to pay *only* the interest for up to five years—referred to as an interest-only loan. I had discovered this back in February when I had used the online loan calculator, but I hadn't really understood what it meant.

Paying only the interest would mean I had to pay far less each month for a few years until the principal payments kicked in. But as most people I knew had gone for a variable home loan, where both the principal and interest were paid, this is what I thought I should choose as well. It would mean I would pay off the loan a bit quicker.

When I had started house-hunting, interest rates had been raised five months in a row after the Reserve Bank had held or reduced them for more than a year. Interest rates had not been moved for two months when I found Treasury Street, but the general consensus was that they were going to go north again as the economy improved in the coming months. However, because the Reserve Bank had reduced the official interest rate to a bargain basement level, the five increases had seen standard variable home loans rates just hit 7.9 per cent at most of the major banks. In any case, Jason had already warned me that I needed to factor in a few interest rate rises when working out what I could afford.

After half a day of research, I could finally insert my details into the bank websites for preliminary pre-approval. When I'd done this, two of the banks said that with a $65 000 income, $38 300 in savings and no other debts, I could borrow around $335 000. This was not going to be enough for me to buy Treasury Street. The Universal Bank website was the more promising. After I had submitted my details, an automated message said I had preliminary pre-approval to borrow $392 000 on a variable home loan where I was paying both principal and interest. With my $38 300 in savings and the $7000 first home owner grant that Jason had mentioned, I would have about $437 300 to spend. This was good, because I had to account for all the additional costs Jason had told me about. It didn't matter to me that Jason said I should look at a loan that was less than 90 per cent of the property purchase price—if the bank wanted to give me that much money, I wasn't going to argue. All I had to do then was wait for someone from Universal to call me to confirm my approval! I wondered if it would be the same woman I had spoke to earlier at the bank. Maybe it is as easy as Max and Jem had said it was going to be! I wanted that house!

Rather than waiting for Universal to ring and approve my loan, I immediately rang the agent handling the sale of the house to put in an offer. I told myself that if I couldn't get the loan within three days I would know it wasn't meant to be. To some people, this may have seemed like a tiny false start, especially after having taken the effort to go into a bank and speak to an adviser, but I was focused on owning Treasury Street and I had turned into a crazy woman with eyes only for the lovely house with the Tuscan courtyard.

I had seen the real estate agent, Simon, on every visit I'd made to Treasury Street, and had also seen him at several other houses I had looked at. To me he looked like he was another smarmy agent in a naff, light-grey suit and cheap, pointy shoes, driving a convertible. I just didn't like the look of him. He also happened to work with my nemesis real estate agent from the false-bidding and toilet-using fiascos. The link should have been enough to tell me to call it quits and walk away with my dignity semi-clad, but still intact. I didn't listen.

Although Simon would have quickly realised my heightened interested in Treasury Street by my constant presence at the open for inspections, I had diligently followed my parents' advice and avoided talking to him after the first time, when he had given me his card. Because of this, when I finally decided to call him, I felt a bit strange about how much I had gone out of my way to avoid him. I was also terrified that his uptight colleague had warned him about my recent escapades and he would say I couldn't have the house based on my poor auction etiquette.

When I introduced myself and said I wanted a copy of the contract, he bluntly asked me how much I was willing to spend. I guess there was no point beating around the bush.

'Three hundred and ninety thousand', I told him. The government consumer website I had read said that when bidding in a private sale the wannabe buyer had to decide whether to put in a bid below the asking price or throw all their cards down and put in their highest offer first up. I chose the former because I desperately wanted to have money left over to afford all the furniture I'd already imagined inside my new house. My plan was foiled immediately.

'There are several other parties interested, so unfortunately you are going to have make a higher bid to stay in the game', he replied snarkily. 'Four hundred thousand would be closer to the mark at this point. You will have to be quick, though; the vendors are already entertaining another offer.'

I told him I would call him back.

I logged onto the Universal Bank website and did some quick sums on the home loan calculator, the stamp duty calculator and the lenders mortgage insurance calculators to see approximately how much extra money I would need to pay all the extras on top of the price of the house. And I was still very conscious of the fact that Jason had said I would need a $5000 buffer.

At least I would be saving money on a lawyer. Alex would definitely help me out for free.

After working it all out, I decided that I could afford to offer more. I'd have a $10 699 as a buffer for interest rate rises, renovations and furniture. It also meant I could put in a higher offer if my first one was rejected.

Purchase property for $401 000	$401 000
Extras (government charges, registration fees, solicitor, insurance etc.)	$25 601
Total cost of purchase	**$426 601**
Home loan (Universal)	$392 000
Savings	$38 300
First home owner grant	$7000
Total funds I can access	**$437 300**
Buffer	**$10 699**

I called Simon back. 'I'd like to put in an offer of $401 000', I said.

'It's close to the end of the day, so I'll courier the contracts out to you in the morning so you can put an offer in writing', Simon replied before asking for my address and hanging up.

Like a new love, I was gushing. I'd completely ignored the fact that I didn't yet have a home loan, but I'd put in an offer and that was all that mattered. And like someone who'd just met the love of her life, I contacted all my friends hoping they would share my excitement, too. But, aside from Max and Jem, they just didn't seem as pleased as I was; especially Eliza.

'What are you doing making offers on houses you don't have the money for?' she sternly asked as soon as I had stopped swooning down the line.

'What do you mean? I've practically got the loan. I'm just waiting for the bank to call me. I haven't signed a contract yet or anything, so I haven't done anything illegal. I've just put in an offer.'

'Oh Maggie, for someone so clever, you can be a real idiot sometimes. This is not the way to buy a home. You need to know exactly what you're getting yourself into and you can't make an offer on a house just because you think it's pretty. This is what I would call a classic example of an emotional purchase.'

'What do you mean?' I said, completely shocked. 'Of course it's emotional; it's going to be my home!'

'Maggie, if you are going to spend $400 000 on a house that backs onto a train line and is the size of a pea, you really need to be certain that it doesn't only look nice on the surface. You need to check out all the details.

'But more importantly, you have to be able to afford it. The Universal website might have told you that you might get a loan, but that's not certain, and you don't even know if you could afford the repayments on that loan!

'You've fallen in love and have rose-tinted glasses on. At least let me look at the paperwork when you get it.'

I wasn't having a bar of anything she said. Eliza always managed to steal my thunder. Surely being emotionally attached to a house couldn't be a bad thing. I was the one who was going to live there, so why shouldn't I love it? That house was going to be mine.

I was still in complete denial about the fact that I hadn't spoken to the bank to actually apply for a loan. But I knew for sure that I certainly wasn't showing Eliza the contract. Alex had already said that he'd go through any contracts with me. I hung up my call to Eliza, cursing myself for having spoken to her about it in the first place.

Alex and I were still spending several nights a week together, but the relationship didn't seem to be progressing past long evenings in his apartment, alone. It was getting close to the end of July and I hadn't met a single one of his friends or anyone in his family, even though he had met many of my friends. He was a busy man, so I decided to go with the flow and tried to not get too attached with the idea of becoming a major part of his life right there and then. Besides, I had a house to think about.

Apart from not meeting his friends, I thought things with us were travelling quite nicely. We had a really good time together. We ate, drank, danced and spent a lot of time in bed. I could see a future for us. Kind of.

I hadn't been able to get onto Alex when I'd called everyone else about the offer I'd made on the house, but later that night I managed to get hold of him on the phone. I told him all about putting in an offer on Treasury Street and how much of a killjoy Eliza had been. Rather than the excitement I'd hoped he'd share with me, I sensed a tone of coolness in his voice that I hadn't heard before. I wondered if I was going to replay my conversation with Eliza.

'That's a big ask', he said in a mocking tone.

'What is?'

'You putting in an offer on a house and not having any finance.'

'I know it is, but I'm sure it will all work out. I should receive the contract from the agent tomorrow. Do you mind having a look?'

I was a little put-out. Wasn't he, of all people, supposed to be supportive? After a few more terse words he agreed to come over for dinner the next day and look over the contract, in return for me cooking him my now-famous tuna and lemon risotto. Since the dinner party I had hosted at Max and Jem's place, Alex had requested the dish three times.

When I hung up the phone and actually sat down and thought about Alex, I realised he had been a little preoccupied the last few times I had seen him. But it had usually worn off after a few minutes and I thought he must have had things on his mind about work. As for me, Alex didn't seem to notice when my mind wandered to thoughts of other things, like Spencer, for instance. Since seeing Spencer at the auction with my father I couldn't quite shake him from my mind. I didn't want him in my life anymore but the more I tried to forget about him, the more he popped into my head. I wondered briefly if one of the reasons I was so keen to see Alex so often was to ward of thoughts of Spencer. The only thought that eased my mind was that if I bought Treasury Street there would be no reason for us to run into each other again when house-hunting.

The contract and a set of papers called the Section 32 arrived the next day just before I was heading out for my lunch break. I had no idea what a Section 32 was, but figured it was all part of the legalities. I called Alex to let him know, and to tee up a time for my romantic dinner—but this time he said would rather meet me at a restaurant near his work at 8.30 that night, saying he had a late meeting and wouldn't be free until then. He still sounded distant and I started to worry that maybe all the obsessing about the house had made me miss something vital to do with our relationship. Or maybe he was annoyed that I'd put in an offer on the house without talking to him first.

The house had also taken my mind off another, slightly important, part of my life: my job. For three weeks I had been doing nothing but living, eating and breathing buying the house. My radio gig was reaping the benefits, but my job at the paper was suffering. I had made two rather large mistakes in my last column and I needed to get back into the land of the living before I lost my dream job and my dream house went out the window with it.

True to form, Janice had been the one to point out that I had put the wrong dates in a column I had written about the Holocaust. I had also accidentally given the new Prime Minister her predecessor's name. Both extremely unprofessional for a journalist and both quickly picked up by my readers who liked to publicly let me and the paper know where we had gone wrong at any opportunity. I wondered whether Janice had noticed the mistakes in the copy for the website, and had let them slip through the net to make me look bad. I wouldn't put it past her.

On the day my paperwork arrived, I had finished my writing for the day and was about to turn off my computer when I noticed a new email in my inbox. It was from my editor.

I started panicking. I had no doubt my editor would have been told about the mistakes I had made in the column and I was sure that was why she was emailing me; she never emailed anyone unless she wanted to talk about something serious.

But surely I wouldn't be fired for making two errors. It wasn't as if I was alone in this; several people would have checked the copy before the paper had gone to print and the website had gone live, and they'd also missed the mistakes.

I couldn't leave without opening the email, but it took me half an hour of staring at the screen to build up the courage to click on it. I was pleasantly surprised.

From: Caroline Eady
Sent: Tuesday, 26 July 4:14 PM
To: Maggie Rose
Subject:

Dear Maggie,

I'm pleased to inform you that Metro TV has requested, and I have approved, your involvement with *The Real Nightly News*. At this stage Metro will not pay you for your appearances, but I have been told there will be opportunities for payment in the future.

Isobel will phone you in the next few days to schedule your involvement with the production meetings.

Congratulations!

Break a leg,
Caroline
Editor
The City

I couldn't believe it. First, because the TV show thing had completely slipped my mind. And second, because the show had already begun to air and the Metro TV producer, Isobel, had not contacted me since my screen test. I was rapt. Things were finally looking up. I had put in an offer on my dream home and my editor and Metro had acknowledged my work.

I raced home to get ready to meet Alex to go through the contracts and tell him my good news. His distance and coolness on the phone were still playing on my mind and I wanted to look good to allay any untoward feelings he was having about seeing me.

I arrived early at the restaurant he had chosen, and drank a glass of champagne at the bar while I waited for him. I wanted to have time to look over the paperwork before he did, so that I knew what he was talking about when he was explaining everything. I quickly looked up a few tricky words on my smartphone ('encumbrances' and 'chattels', anyone?) so that I didn't have to feel stupid by asking him what every second word meant.

Alex hadn't shown up by 8.45, so I sent him a text message to check that I was in the right place. When he hadn't returned my text five minutes later, I tried to call him but his phone was turned off.

He wouldn't be standing me up, would he?

I sat at the bar for another 30 minutes, anxiously skimming the contract while trying to look nonchalant. I must have called his phone four times before giving up and leaving. I hoped nothing had happened to him, but from the tone of his voice earlier I had a feeling that his absence had more to do with our relationship and less to do with him lying injured in a gutter somewhere. I had no idea why he just wouldn't have said that he couldn't catch up rather than leaving me sitting at the bar feeling desperate and dateless. I also needed him to explain the contract and I wanted to have it signed and delivered to the agent the next day.

When I arrived home I kept studying the paperwork while I waited for Alex to return my calls and explain himself. It felt strange, though, that I wasn't beside myself with worry about his wellbeing. I somehow had a feeling that nothing bad had happened to him; that his standing me up was actually about us. I feel asleep at midnight.

When Alex still hadn't rung the next morning, instead of calling the police, I became really angry. I tried his phone again and it was still turned off. As soon as I got into the office, I checked my emails to see if he had sent me anything that might explain where he was. There was nothing from Alex but there was a voice message left on my work phone from Simon the real estate agent.

The message was from 6.30 the night before—he'd left it after I left the office—and he was asking whether I could increase my offer on Treasury Street to $410 000. I sat at my desk and stared at the contract and, on another complete whim, decided to just increase my bid by $9000 and sign the contract.

What was another $9000, really, over a 30-year loan? I wouldn't have much of a buffer, but I was sure that would work itself out over time.

I had gained little understanding in all my studying of the contract the night before—in fact, being so distracted by thoughts of Alex, I really hadn't understood much at all. And I hadn't even looked at the document called the Section 32 yet. But these people weren't out to trick me. It was a property contract, not a tax return! I was sure everything would be above board.

I had looked at the government consumer website, though, and the one thing I did know from that was that I should make sure the contract stated that my offer was conditional on me getting finance. So I included that when I signed. I wasn't too concerned that no-one from the bank had contacted me since I lodged my application for pre-approval—it had only been four days and I was sure they had a backlog to get through. I made a copy of the contract and then called Simon back. By 11 am he had sent a courier to my office to pick up the paperwork. It all happened in such a whirlwind that it didn't seem real.

At lunchtime that day I went to a local café with Genevieve. I needed to rehash what had happened with Alex and I was looking forward to telling her all about finding my dream home in Treasury Street. Genevieve had been home visiting her family in Scotland for a month, and there was a lot to catch up on in her life as well. She had run into an old flame while home and had fallen in love.

'Okay, tell me if this is weird', I said to Genevieve as we sat down. 'Things had been going gangbusters with Alex and I, and then last night he stands me up and tells me nothing. Nada. Zip. I haven't heard from him at all.

He seemed like the perfect guy and then this! Honestly, the only thing that had seemed wrong was that he had sounded distant on the phone yesterday and was maybe a bit cool the other day. But he still arranged to have dinner with me last night and he had never given any indication that he wasn't happy with how things were going. I just can't believe that he would stand me up and not have the decency to at least give me a courtesy call to explain.' I had very quickly made myself angry all over again, talking about Alex. This rant escaped my mouth in a matter of seconds.

Genevieve was more sympathetic towards him. 'That's very strange, Maggie—but are you sure nothing has happened to him? Have you called his work? Or the local hospitals?'

'I thought about calling the police', I told her, 'but I'm certain he's okay.' Of course, having Genevieve's voice of reason in my ear made me think I probably should call someone else to check that he wasn't in trouble. Maybe I was being a bit heartless.

While we waited for our sandwiches and coffees to arrive, I called Alex's law firm. I asked to speak to him and the receptionist said he was out of the office. Well, at least he wasn't in a hospital. My conscience eased somewhat.

When the receptionist asked if I wanted to leave a message, I was forced to explain who I was and why I was calling. She said he'd left for London the night before and wouldn't be back for a fortnight!

Once again I could feel the steam hissing from my ears as I hung up and told Genevieve what the receptionist had said.

'I am furious!' I couldn't contain myself. 'What the hell does he think he's doing? You'd think after all this fooling around for the past six months he'd have the decency to let me know he was leaving the country.'

'I know, Maggie. I'm as perplexed as you', Genevieve soothed. 'You really do have bad luck with men. Hey, let's go out tonight. You look as though you need a stiff drink. I haven't even had a chance to tell you about Mac. He's thinking about moving here.'

I felt awful and selfish turning Genevieve down, as all we'd talked about over lunch was my problems with Alex, and I wanted to hear about Mac and also tell her about being offered a place on the TV show. But I had no choice. 'I'm sorry, but I can't tonight. I need to save as much money as I can. I've just signed a contract to buy a $410 000 house.' As the words escaped my mouth, reality set in. I started sweating.

'You WHAT?' Genevieve screamed, but I barely heard her.

'And I don't have the money to buy it! Oh my goodness, what have I done?' I was now in full-blown freak-out mode.

It was time to admit to myself that I was making a massive mistake and could not buy Treasury Street. I had fallen so thoroughly in love with the place that common sense had been thrown out the window. There was no avoiding the fact that I didn't have a loan, and I was no closer to getting a loan than I was a week ago when I didn't even know what a variable interest rate was. I had convinced myself that actually talking to a bank about a real loan application was the scariest thing in the world. What did I think I was doing? I had saved more than $38 500 by then, but that didn't mean anything without the loan! I could feel Treasury Street slipping away as I sat staring at Genevieve across the table, a look of shock on my face.

I didn't want to have to call Eliza, but I had no choice. I needed her to look at the contract I'd signed to make sure I hadn't royally screwed up my entire life on a whim. I had actually studied the government's consumer website before putting in the offer, but as I wasn't a lawyer, and my knowledge of reading contracts was minimal. I was more than nervous—I was terrified.

On the way back from lunch, with Genevieve still trying to soothe me, I rang Eliza's mobile. I told her what had happened with the house and Alex. She didn't bite my head off; instead, she told me to come to her place as soon as I had finished work with my copy of the contract.

I spent the rest of the day sweating at my desk, while trying to concentrate on my work and prepare my column. I was having such trouble concentrating on the task at hand, and when Isobel from Metro rang about my guest spot on *The Real Nightly News* and I was once again thrown into disarray. Isobel said the executive producer wanted me to sit on the show's panel for about 15 minutes of the hour-long program about once every fortnight or so. It seemed like a long time for me to be on air with absolutely no experience—but actually it was only two segments between ad breaks. I asked her what they were going to get me to talk about, and she said most of that would be decided on the day of the show. I was scheduled to sit in on a production meeting at the end of the week.

As soon as I finished work, I forwent my usual penny-pinching and jumped in a taxi and headed straight to Eliza's place. She had sent her husband out for the night with their baby so we could concentrate on the latest disaster in my life.

'Just tell me I haven't signed my life away', I said once she put on her glasses and sat down at the kitchen table to read the paperwork. I was pacing up and down the room wringing my hands.

'Pour yourself a glass of wine and go and sit in the other room while I read this', Eliza ordered. 'I can't focus with you anywhere near me.'

My life was in Eliza's hands, or so it seemed to me. I had no idea what had possessed me to make an offer on a house I didn't have the money to buy. I may have been bad with money in the past, but I had come a long way since then, and this seemed totally out of character. I told myself that if Eliza could not help me I was going to leave the country the next day and start a new life in Buenos Aires.

Ten minutes later, Eliza called for me to come back into the kitchen. She sounded serious. I made my way down the hallway with my feet feeling as heavy as lead blocks and my palms sweating in anticipation of what was about to unfold.

'Maggie, you can calm down now', Eliza's tone was a little softer now. 'You have done the right thing by writing that the contract is conditional on you getting finance. You're well within your rights to simply retract the offer.'

I was so relieved I ran over and threw my arms around her. 'Thank you. Thank you. Thank you!' I gushed, smothering Eliza and the contract in my embrace.

'Now, can you please tell me what is wrong with you?' Eliza said, pushing me away and holding me at arm's length, looking sternly into my face. 'What are you trying to do to yourself? Is this about seeing Spencer around?' Eliza always had a special way of getting to the point, and motherhood hadn't softened her one bit. But her eyes told me she was concerned rather than angry.

'I don't know. Seeing Spencer around at the auctions probably didn't help...but no, it wasn't the reason I did it. I'm just really sick of missing out on houses all the time. I've been looking for so long—it's just not fair.'

'Maggie, you've only been looking at houses for six months. It can take some people years to find a house that's within their budget. Do you even know what your budget is?'

'Well, Jason told me I would probably be able to borrow around $380 000, but then the Universal Bank's website gave me pre-approval for more than $390 000. I figured that with that loan and my savings, I could still buy the place for $410 000. I really wanted the house and I thought it would all fall into place and the bank would be fine with everything.'

'But Maggie, you haven't even been to a bank to see if and how much they will *actually* lend you yet!'

'I have been to a bank. I just didn't apply for a loan.' I was being facetious, I knew. But it was a defence. Eliza was right. All I had was the preliminary pre-approval, based on a few questions on a website. I didn't have the loan— I may or may not be able to get the loan, but the fact was that I was making an offer without formally knowing if I could actually afford it. It really did seem a bit stupid.

I promised Eliza I wouldn't do anything this rash again and she offered to write a letter retracting my offer on Treasury Street. Feeling slightly better about the housing situation and having Eliza back on my side, we drank some more wine and I told her about getting a gig on the TV show. Then we tried to nut out what had gone wrong with Alex. Despite knowing him for several years while at university, Eliza had nothing to offer me by way of insight into why he would have gone overseas without a word to the girl he was supposed to be in a relationship with.

'It doesn't sound too promising, does it?' I finally admitted.

We stayed up until 1 am and I spent the night on Eliza's couch.

She was already awake and writing the formal letter to the real estate agent when I woke up at 7 am the next day. She then faxed the retraction to Simon for me and I told her I would call my bank manager to make an appointment for some time in the coming weeks to talk for real about getting a loan. I kissed her goodbye and rushed off to the radio station, privately thanking the gods that I had such a lovely friend.

Although the wounds of the past few days were still raw for me, Darren, the radio station disk jockey, loved my real estate and romantic horror stories. I changed the name of the street and the agent and gave a five-minute rundown on how not to buy a house through a private sale. He particularly enjoyed the part where I told him I had been stood up be my lawyer boyfriend and decided to go ahead and sign the contract anyway.

I didn't intend to bring up Alex on air but I was annoyed with him and I felt really hurt. I left his name out to protect his identity and, as he was in London, I thought there was no chance of him hearing my segment.

As had become par for the course, Angelica continued to send me daggers from the producer's booth. Although I tried to ignore her, there were moments when I found myself staring at her like a stunned mullet, and when she caught me she'd give me a weird knowing smile. It was very off-putting. But I daresay every woman has found herself unwittingly staring at her ex-boyfriend's new girlfriend. It's the 'what does he see in her?' stare.

Unfortunately, although a heinous bitch, Angelica was extremely good-looking—maybe that's what he saw in her. I certainly didn't cut the mustard in comparison.

As I was leaving the station that day, I heard her mutter something under her breath in my direction. I might have been wrong, but I thought I heard her say something like, 'You know what they say: unlucky in love…' I missed the end of her sentence as I was more focused on getting the hell out of there than actually listening to anything she had to say.

There is no way to describe how much Angelica annoyed me. But her parting words made me realise that she had absolutely no tact. I couldn't figure out why Spencer was going out with such a half-wit.

On the way to work from the radio station I started to think there may have been some truth in what Eliza had said about running into Spencer being the reason I had developed an intense emotional attachment to the Treasury Street. Aside from being a way to make sure I didn't continue to run into him, there was no other reason I could come up with to explain why I had turned into a stark, raving lunatic who was making offers on houses without having the money to pay. It was utter madness. The house was lovely, but it *did* look over a train line and *was* rather small.

I managed to get through the rest of the day relatively unscathed, though I had been slightly late in handing in my column. I'd heard nothing more from Simon the agent since the retraction of my offer that morning and, more importantly, Alex still hadn't made any contact.

When I got home that night, I sat and looked at my small room in someone else's house and was devastated that I really couldn't own Treasury Street. I didn't want to have to get back out on the house-hunting trail. It was all proving to be too hard.

I also felt like an idiot for putting any faith in a man who had a history of going overseas for weeks at a time but didn't even having the decency to call me while he was away. Based on that, why would I be surprised by his current behaviour?

The next morning Janice berated me in front of the entire newsroom for handing in my column late the previous day, saying it had held up production on the website. She then warned me never to do it again or she would have to inform the editor of my lax attitude. There was once a time when I thought there was a minute chance that Janice and I could be friends, but over the past couple of years I had realised it was never going to happen. Between her and Angelica, I had had enough of strange, bitchy women who felt they could talk to me like I was some kind of an idiot. I was sick to death of both them.

To end what had been possibly my worst week since Spencer left for Japan without me, I reluctantly headed to Monovale to the Metro Studios to sit in on a production meeting. I had been running late for work that morning and hadn't been able to dedicate much time to my clothes or hair; I looked a right mess. My hair was messily piled on top of my head. A button had popped off my new shirt (I had put on a tiny bit of weight) and I hadn't had time to repair it, so my old bra was visible. My pants had a hole in the side that I'd forgotten to sew up the night before. All in all, I wasn't looking my spunkiest.

After my previous trip to the studio where I had turned up looking more like a drag queen than the fresh-faced 'bright young thing' they had wanted to recruit, I had decided to forget about wearing any make-up. I regretted that decision as soon I sat in the back of the taxi on the way to the studio, and spent the ride scouring my bag for any make-up I may have left in there. All I could find was the remnants of a slightly crusty favourite red lipstick and a new mascara Mum had given me before I went to New York, which I had forgotten about. Despite not being able to find a mirror in my bag, I slapped on the make-up and checked my teeth for lipstick in the dull reflection of the taxi window. There was nothing else I could do but hope for the best.

Isobel was waiting for me in the lobby and was as lovely as the first time we met. She took me for a coffee in the Metro cafeteria to brief me on what to expect at the production meeting, explaining who was going to be there. I still felt intimidated by the whole situation; I'd watched a few episodes of the program and couldn't imagine myself being on the show at all.

Isobel explained that this was a production meeting to go over the previous night's show and begin planning for the next week's show. The two hosts, Benjamin and Celia, would be in the meeting, as well as the executive producer and his minions, and the screen writers. A news producer would also be there to make sure the news agenda was kept fresh. Isobel said I wouldn't have to do much except sit and listen, and that I wouldn't be expected to contribute anything. I probably wouldn't be involved in these types of meetings regularly—it was more important that I attended my pre-show meetings when necessary. She said she'd introduce me to everyone when we got to the meeting and reassured me they were all excited that I was coming on board. As we got up to leave, I jokingly asked her if they would mind that I looked like such a mess.

'You look fabulous—what are you talking about?' was her response.

I could tell she meant it and I almost started crying with gratitude that someone had said something nice to me. I wanted to be Isobel's friend, but I also wanted her to take me back to the make-up room where Madeleine had so expertly done my face and hair for my screen test.

We were the first to arrive in the meeting room and we sat in the farthest corner from the door. I was nervous and still had no real idea of what I was up for. Benjamin, one of the hosts, was the first of the others to arrive, and Isobel introduced us.

'Good to have you on the team, Maggie. I've heard a lot of good things about you', Benjamin said.

Benjamin was a former comedy star who had developed a taste for politics and decided to base his entire career around talking about how awful politicians were. It was good to meet him too, except that I was a little uneasy about these 'good things' he said he'd heard, and who he could have heard them from.

Isobel seemed different around Benjamin. She seemed almost nervous, which to scruffy old me seemed strange for such a stunning and confident woman. I didn't detect any nervous vibes from Benjamin, but I then I had never met him before in my life and the only time I had ever laid eyes on him was on a TV screen at home.

After Benjamin, I was introduced to his co-host, Celia, and a cavalcade of producers and writers. Finally I met the executive producer, who had created the show.

The meeting started with the executive producer giving everyone a dressing down for the previous night's program. Apparently there had been several stuff-ups on the production front, though I'd watched the show and I hadn't noticed. But I wasn't exactly a television production aficionado, was I? The executive producer was about to launch into the agenda for the next week's show when he paused, looked up and scanned the faces at the table.

'Where's Spencer?' he asked the room.

My blood pressure instantly went through the roof at the sound of Spencer's name. But maybe it was a different Spencer. Surely there had to be more than one Spencer in this city. Oh, who was I kidding? Trying to deceive myself never worked.

A producer said she'd go and find him and the meeting continued. Not for me, though. My mouth went dry and I started to feel claustrophobic. I could feel my skin getting hot and hear my pulse in my ears. I was breathing so heavily that I thought the other shirt buttons across my chest were at risk of shooting off across the room and hitting the executive producer in the head. Isobel looked at me and asked me if I was okay, and I told her I needed some fresh air. I felt as if I was having an anxiety attack. I needed to put my head between my legs but I didn't think that was going to impress anyone.

I took myself to the bathroom and splashed water on my face to try and cool myself down. I went into a cubicle and sat down to calm myself. When my breathing slowed, I realised I needed to get back into the meeting. I wanted to freshen up a little, so applied some more mascara as I sat in the cubicle. I was so frazzled that I didn't even have the presence of mind to use the bathroom mirror. I felt tears forming in my eyes, but I needed to forge ahead. Even if it was the same Spencer, I couldn't let him stop me from furthering my career. Pulling myself together, I walked back to the meeting room.

Without making eye contact with anyone, I marched to my seat and sat down. Isobel was making notes and didn't look up when I returned. I slowly lifted my head to see that, yes, it was *my* Spencer who was now seated next to the executive producer. The two were deep in conversation. Spencer looked up and smiled at me before double-taking and giving me a strange look. Spencer had started to grow a beard since the last time we had run into one another and it suited him. Then the executive producer noticed me and gave me another strange look. It registered with me but I didn't take any notice. Putting on a brave face took all my strength.

I sat silent through the rest of the meeting while trying to stop myself from looking at Spencer. I was told that my role on the show would be to talk about what was setting the news agenda that week. It was almost identical to my spot on Freedom AM, but for one thing …

'Spencer, our news director, will take you through your paces the night before the show', Michael said before concluding the meeting.

A fortnightly one-on-one with Spencer? Could things get any worse? I wondered if he'd bring Angelica just to make it all the more tortuous for me.

As Isobel walked me to the entrance of the building she turned and gave me a serious look.

'I hate to tell you this now, Maggie, but you have mascara running all the way down your cheeks.'

'What? Why didn't you tell me?' I gasped, horrified, wiping at my face.

'I didn't notice until we left the meeting. It wasn't there when you arrived.'

'How embarrassing!' I cried. 'I splashed water on my face and then reapplied mascara in the bathroom when I took a break during the meeting. Oh, no—I didn't even look in the mirror! No wonder the producer and Spencer were looking at me so weirdly.'

I turned to once again look for a bathroom, only to see Spencer racing down the corridor towards us.

'Maggie, wait', he called breathlessly.

I wanted to run. I had no idea how silly I must look, having no doubt now smeared the mascara right across my cheeks when I wiped at them. I braced myself and pretended there was nothing wrong.

'Spencer, how're you going? I guess we'll be working together again.'

Isobel must have sensed there was some sort of tension between us, as she said her goodbyes and told me she'd be in touch the next week.

'I'm really sorry I didn't tell you I was working on the show', he said once we were alone.

I could tell he was sincere. I didn't want him to think I had a problem with seeing him, so I smiled and told him it was fine, and that I was looking forward to working with him on the show. He seemed relieved, as if he'd been worried about my feelings. Although I found that hard to believe.

'I'll see you next week, then', I said to him as I backed away. He looked so good. It wasn't fair.

'I'll give you a call next week to arrange a time for us to meet next Wednesday. Isobel will also be there.' He turned to walk away, paused, then turned back. 'Um, also, I think you have mascara all over your cheeks.'

With my face clean but still feeling like I had egg on it, I headed straight to a bar in Leighton to meet Genevieve, Fran, Tim, Max and Jem.

'This week has to go down in the annals of history as one of your worst on record', Max said. 'It almost beats the time Fran and Tim evicted you for not paying your rent after you had spent five days in a car, alone, on a stakeout.' They all laughed hysterically.

'What was it that Angelica said to you? "Unlucky in love"?' Genevieve asked.

'Does anyone have any idea what that quote means?' I asked.

Fran Googled the quote on her phone and read it out. '"Lucky in cards, unlucky in love." Apparently you must be good at card games, then. Or something.'

'Oh, who knows what the woman was talking about', I laughed, feeling good that I could see the funny side of it.

'Who cares what she thinks of you, anyway? You're going to be a TV star', the ever-supportive Genevieve continued. 'How do you think she's going to react when she finds out you're working with Spencer? Do you think he got you the job?'

I didn't care about Angelica or Spencer anymore and I knew without asking that my editor had organised the job. The worries of the week were washed away as my friends and I talked and sang the night away at our favourite bar. I felt as though I'd come home. The past seven months had been a roller-coaster of house-hunting, Alex leaving and Spencer making his way back into my life. I just wanted my life to return to normal.

On his insistence that I get straight back on the horse, my dad picked me up the next morning to take me to two inspections in a suburb called Hornville. Hornville was 15 kilometres out of the city and nowhere near where I wanted to live. I wasn't what you would have called enthusiastic, but I humoured my father and went along with him. One consolation was that I didn't think there was any chance of running into anyone I knew there.

The first house Dad had found was a two-bedroom 1950s clinker brick unit. It shared a party wall with an identical place next door. The décor was incredibly outdated, but it was big and close to public transport and a couple of nice coffee shops. It was on the market for $410 000. I hadn't thought about buying a unit and it made me feel a little like I was turning into a spinster, destined to make a life for just one person. I also didn't know anyone who lived nearby and I told Dad I would feel too isolated if I lived that far out of the city. I told him I didn't want to see the second place as the whole experience was depressing me.

'I just want you to see that there are other options. It's a big city and you shouldn't confine your search to three suburbs. You'll miss out on something if you don't expand your horizons a little.'

'Dad, I know what I'm doing now. I'm going to make an appointment to see my bank manager in a few weeks' time.' I wasn't quite ready to go back to the bank just yet, so hadn't yet made the appointment.

'But honestly, Dad, I'm really ready to give up. I don't even think there's any point going to the bank. They probably won't lend me the money, anyway.'

We drove back to my parents' place and Mum had lunch waiting for us. My Aunt Lily was there for lunch, too, and I sat at the table and told them that I wanted to give up.

'Don't be disheartened, Maggie', Mum said.

'You know', Aunt Lily chimed in, 'I have a good friend whose husband is a buyer's advocate.' She said this as though I knew exactly what she was talking about. 'He might be able to help you out.'

When I looked at her blankly, she explained that a buyer's advocate is a property expert, but rather than working for the person selling a house, like a real estate agent does, an advocate works in the best interests of the person looking to buy. They know the best places to buy and will advise on how much a buyer should be spending.

'At the very least, he'll point you in the right direction', Aunt Lily said.

***

The next week rolled on and I still hadn't heard a word from Alex. Spencer, on the other hand, had called me twice to arrange our pre-show meeting. Both conversations were awkward and essentially futile as he could have sent me a text telling me what time to show up instead of making us both feel weird about talking on the phone to each other. I had to meet him at the TV studios on the Wednesday to go through my role. I felt better knowing Isobel was going to be with us, but I was still nervous about seeing him. I didn't know how I was going to act like a normal person when there was so much history between us.

I arrived at Metro TV right on time and, once again, Isobel was waiting for me in the lobby. She walked me back towards the room where the production meeting had taken place, but turned off into another corridor and stopped when we got to a door with Spencer's name on it. There was no-one in the office, but she went inside and beckoned me to follow.

'I thought Spencer worked as the news director of the news room', I said to Isobel while we waited in his office for him to arrive.

'He does, but he's also news director for the current affairs arm.' She looked over at me. 'You seem a little uncomfortable. Are you nervous?'

'Um, Spencer is my ex-boyfriend. We don't really talk, so this is very awkward for me.'

'I wondered how he knew you so well. Look, if you know Spencer, then you know you don't need to feel uncomfortable. He's right behind you being on the show', Isobel said as Spencer walked in the room.

I didn't know how I would bring myself to look up and say hello to him. I wanted to know what he had said to Isobel about me. But, taking a deep breath, I sat up in my chair and said hello like a professional.

'Good to see you again, Maggie', he said. 'Let's get down to business. I have to be in another meeting in 30 minutes.'

I was glad I knew how long the torture was going to last—I thought I'd be able to make it through 30 minutes. Spencer sat down at his desk and told me that Benjamin the host would have a news list to stick to on the show. That week's show was going to focus on the recent revolution and youth uprising in Egypt, the upcoming state election and a couple of other less important issues. Spencer said I would only be on the show for about 10 or 15 minutes and then I would be free to leave. He acted as though he didn't know me at all. It was strictly business.

Throughout the meeting I maintained eye contact with the wall behind his head, carefully avoiding meeting his blue eyes. It was nothing short of bizarre to be sitting in a small room with him and for nothing to be said about the past. Of course he was at work, Isobel was there, and I had not been particularly warm to him so far, but I was expecting him to joke around a little. He clearly wanted to get the meeting over and done with and get away from me as fast as he could.

We left the office and Isobel asked if I wanted to grab a drink with her. I needed to calm down and said yes. It took me just one drink before I blurted out everything that had happened between Spencer and me. I never once mentioned Alex, who for all I knew could come home next week and have a perfectly good explanation for deserting me.

Isobel listened intently as I ranted on about myself and I soon realised I had become completely self-obsessed. I changed the subject and started asking Isobel about her life. As well as being beautiful, Isobel was also an accomplished journalist who had won several major awards for breaking news. She was single—something I could not believe—and by the third drink she told me she was desperately in love from afar with Benjamin, the host of *The Real Nightly News.*

Full of bravado, I told her I'd help her win Benjamin's heart if my life depended on it. We were acting like 16 year old's, not like the 32-year-old women we both were. We had become friends, and the pair of us sat at the bar for four hours before stumbling out to find taxis close to midnight.

The next morning was a nightmare. At my regular radio spot, Angelica informed me she would be sitting in the front row of the audience for the filming of *The Real Nightly News* that night. At the paper, I struggled to research my next column and prepare for my blog; I was completely beside myself with stress about going on live TV that night. To top it all off, I looked awfully hung-over and had stupidly weighed myself that morning to discovered I had put on three kilograms since I'd weighed myself a few months earlier. All perfect timing for my confidence level!

Isobel said I was to be at the station at 4.30 that afternoon for a pre-show production meeting with Spencer and the executive producer. I sat in the meeting listening intently to the plan for the show before Spencer took me aside and gave me another brief talk about what I was expected to do. I really didn't need to say much, he said. I was there to let the audience know the breaking stories and also talk about what was being reported in the newspapers about the news issues raised on the show. And I would have a teleprompter for much of what I would be saying. Even so, I had spent two hours after lunch that day brushing up on the topics so that I could ad-lib with the rest of the cast during filming.

After the meeting, I headed into hair and make-up, where I found Isobel nursing a coffee. Madeleine the make-up artist was finishing up the co-host Celia's hair and I sat back and chatted to the three of them while I waited for my turn in the chair. When it was my go, Madeleine crafted an incredibly chic and sleek bun on the top of my head and gave me severe black eye make-up. I looked a million times better than when I had walked in. But I just didn't quite feel as tickety-boo as I should have; my confidence level was still at ankle-height.

Next up was the wardrobe department, where I was put into a red strapless dress that was as un-news-like as I could imagine, but it looked great and hugged my curves to perfection. I was suddenly feeling much more comfortable in my skin, with a great outfit to compliment the extra kilos I had gained. I was also wearing a pair of stilettos and by the time I left the wardrobe department I could barely walk due to the tight dress and killer heels. I left the department and walked straight into Spencer who almost knocked me over in his haste to get past.

'Maggie! I didn't recognise you', he said, sounding completely back to his old self again. 'You look incredible. Red's always been your colour.' He was holding my shoulders to steady me as he spoke and I could see he was blushing.

His hands felt so familiar that it was scary. As I looked at him I realised that I liked his beard. And there was that tiny scar on his cheek that I remembered...I needed to get out of there!

'Thanks', was all I could muster as I twisted to get out of his grasp. But even though I desperately wanted to pretend he didn't exist, I couldn't help smiling.

'Are you ready to go on? You'd better head into the green room to meet up with the rest of the guys from the show.'

I scooted off without another word.

After a few minutes in the green room chatting to Celia about the latest supermodel's drug scandal, we were told to make our way out onto the set. The first person I saw was Gabe Levine, the State Government's health minister, who was sitting on the panel between Benjamin and the seat where I had been told to sit. I had no idea there was going to be a politician on the show with us. Why wouldn't they have told me that?

Gabe Levine was generally known as a lecherous fool. He had made a right mess of the state's health system and the year before I had heard whispers of some kind of a sex scandal from my colleagues who worked the political beat. I sat down next to him and introduced myself as professionally as I could muster.

'Yes, Maggie Rose, you work for *The City*. I don't get into the lighter opinion pieces that often', he said, before looking me up and down sleazily and then turning his back to me to have his make-up touched up.

The adrenaline was pumping through my veins and when the show went live to air I was raring to go. Benjamin introduced everyone and it was only then that I looked up at the audience and saw Angelica sitting front and centre, staring at me viciously, with Spencer sitting next to her. I concentrated on what Benjamin and Celia were saying and smiled at the camera like a Stepford wife, while in my peripheral vision Angelica continued to give me daggers.

When Benjamin turned to me to ask me about the latest breaking news, I went to open my mouth to talk and all that came out was a stutter. I composed myself, refocused on the teleprompter, took a deep breath and started again.

> **THE TOP STORY**
>
> **TODAY IS FROM**
>
> **EGYPT, WHERE**
>
> **STUDENTS HAVE**
>
> **HELPED OVERTURN**
>
> **THE 30-YEAR**
>
> **DICTATORSHIP ...**

The camera I was supposed to look into was directly in Angelica's line of fire and she was sitting there smugly with a smile as wide as the Cheshire Cat's. But with my first minute of scripted dialogue now out the way, I was able to relax and listen to what my cohorts were actually saying, and join in on the discussion.

It was then that Gabe Levine's clammy hand brushed the side of my leg. I sat bolt upright in my chair from shock. I thought for a second that it had just been an accident, but as I snuck a look at him out of the corner of my eye I could see him looking at me lecherously and smiling his sleazy smile.

I desperately tried to ignore him and keep up with the panel's conversation, which had now moved from the revolution to the state of the health system and our ability to manage crises. I had written a piece about this earlier in the year and I was just waiting for my time to chime in when that clammy hand suddenly came sliding onto my thigh, just above my knee. I couldn't help it—I squealed and jerked my leg away!

He retracted his hand straight away, but the damage was done. I was furious and, worst of all, the whole panel was looking at me.

'Maggie?' Benjamin said. 'Have you got something to add? This seems like an issue that you're really passionate about.'

'Actually Benjamin, yes, it is—but more importantly it's an issue that our esteemed and *honourable* health minister should be passionate about', I said, turning towards the horrible Gabe Levine. 'Because perhaps if he were paying more attention to his portfolio rather than playing nice with the public, we wouldn't be in this disgraceful situation.'

Steeling myself, I launched into a strangely succinct spiel about how the health system needed billions of dollars pumped into training new doctors and nurses; all of it aimed at the vile man sitting next to me. I didn't give him a chance to speak or squirm his way out of the truths I was espousing. I simply wrapped up my points and handed the floor back to the hosts.

'Thanks, Maggie', said Celia, turning back to face the camera with a smile on her face. 'Coming up after the break ...'

Isobel was waiting for me in the green room when I walked in from the set during the ad break. I was exhilarated. I gave her the rundown of the politician's hand-groping and we sat there laughing together as we watched the rest of the show and noticed that, in a sweet twist of fate, he had visible wet patches under his arms, as he had been sweating profusely under the lights and the intensity of further questioning he was now getting from the rest of the panel.

When the show had wrapped, Isobel said I *had* to go to the post-filming party at a local bar. I couldn't refuse — I had drunkenly promised to help her win over Benjamin, after all.

Everyone from the show was at the bar and it wasn't long before I was in the vicinity of Spencer and Angelica, who were talking with Benjamin and a few other people. As I was on a mission to get Isobel and Benjamin together, I didn't think it was fair to Isobel if I ran screaming in the direction of the toilet to hide in a cubicle. I told Isobel that if we just hung around nearby, Benjamin was certain to get bored with the conversation and we could swoop on him.

For someone who had no connection with the show except through her boyfriend, Angelica seemed to be the life of the party. She had her arm around some bloke I'd never laid eyes on, while shamelessly flirting with Benjamin at the same time. I couldn't believe it. Spencer was standing right next to her and she had the gall to be all over someone else.

After 15 minutes, Benjamin was finally on his own and I grabbed his arm to come and talk to Isobel and myself. Benjamin cracked some lame jokes that weren't at all funny. Isobel laughed awkwardly and I took that as my cue to excuse myself and head for the bar. While I was waiting to be served, Spencer appeared next to me. I quickly glanced around to make sure his mad girlfriend wasn't next to him.

'You were great tonight, Maggie', he said genuinely.

'Thanks, Spencer. That really means a lot.' And I really meant it.

'How's the house-hunting going? Angelica said you'd run into a few problems.'

I groaned on the inside. I was not going to give Spencer a rundown of the dramas with Treasury Street, so I lied and simply told him everything was going to plan.

'How about you two?' I asked changing the focus of the conversation. 'Have you bought a place yet?'

'I'm not buying a house, Maggie. Angelica is looking for one for herself. I moved back in with my old housemate who I was living with before I left for Japan. He was so disorganised that he never got another roommate.'

'I just thought, because you were always at the auctions together, you were buying a place. My mistake', I said, as I attempted to stop myself beaming from ear to ear with the news.

I wanted to run around the room and holler with joy. I was so relieved that he wasn't about to move in and start a life with Angelica. It didn't change the fact that he was going out with her, but the thought of Spencer settling down with Angelica had sent shivers down my spine. I calmed myself down and offered to buy him a drink. I was suddenly sick of being cold to him all the time.

As we talked, it was just like old times, minus any physical contact. He hadn't changed one bit. He was still serious, with a goofy side. The rest of the bar seemed not to exist while we talked. I couldn't stop smiling and he didn't take his eyes off me for a moment.

We stood together for close to 20 minutes before Angelica barrelled up to find him.

'Spencer, I want you to take me home now', she drunkenly purred in his ear.

'Angelica, give me a minute. I'm just catching up with Maggie.'

'I can see that', she said, suddenly sounding a lot more sober. Spencer shrugged free of her embrace and Angelica stormed off, having completely ignored me.

Spencer didn't go after her; instead, he turned back to talk to me. I was glad he hadn't given in. After seeing Angelica slobbering all over Benjamin and another guy earlier, my worst thoughts about her being a horrible person were once again confirmed.

'Sorry about that. She's a bit wrecked.' He looked a bit defeated.

'No need to apologise to me at all. You'd better go. I need to find Isobel, anyway.'

'I'm so happy to get to spend time with you again, Maggie', Spencer said as he leaned in to kiss me on the cheek. I turned away to avoid his kiss, pretending I was looking for someone. I really did want to kiss him, but as long as he was with Angelica, our relationship would be strictly professional.

The party had started to get rowdy. I left Spencer at the bar and went to see how Isobel was going with Benjamin. I spotted Benjamin, but Isobel seemed to have left. Thinking it was also a good time for me to leave, I said my goodbyes and headed home.

On the train back to my little rented room I felt sad about all the strange things that had been happening to me. The buzz I had felt after the show that evening had faded. Seeing Spencer with that idiot was plain awful, and I still didn't have a house, much less a loan.

'I am going to succeed and get this house if it's the last thing I ever do', I said aloud, hoping it would sink in.

My housemates were still up when I arrived at my place. They had both watched the show and said they thought I'd looked and sounded pretty good for a first timer. I walked into my room and there was an enormous bunch of roses sitting on my dresser.

'Who are the flowers from?' I asked as I walked back into the lounge room. Julia and James didn't know, but James said a courier had delivered them earlier that evening. I returned to my room to look for a card. They were from Alex.

> *Maggie, I'm sorry. I'll explain everything and make it up to you when I get back in a couple of weeks.*
>
> *Alex x*

After not one phone call, text message or email in more than a week, Alex had deigned to send me flowers. I was not impressed.

***

Life resumed as normal after that night for the next month or so. I concentrated on writing my columns and blogs, and doing my radio and TV gigs. My second appearance on TV had gone well and had been fun, even though in our production meeting Spencer had passed on a few stern words from the show's producer about trying not to humiliate politicians live on air—apparently the producer didn't think this was okay! I'd had doubts about my future with the show if I wasn't going to be allowed to speak my mind, but I decided I could tone it down while still getting my message across. Spencer was good about the whole thing and we'd been speaking to each other almost normally after our chat at the wrap party on my first night. We were by no means best friends, but we seemed to be getting along civilly.

As much as I had enjoyed acting almost normally around Spencer, though, I didn't really want to put myself through having to see him more than once a week. I asked if it would be alright if we caught up for our briefing on the day the TV show went to air, rather than the night before. This way I only had to see him on the night of the show. I did a further two shows this way without any more wandering-hand- or Angelica-related problems.

Alex called several times when he returned from London and I didn't answer; I didn't want to speak to him. On one of the voice messages he had left on my mobile since he had returned, he said he had been asked to fly to London at the last minute to oversee a big real estate deal and had completely forgotten about our date in the rush to get to the airport on time. He went on to say that he'd been in London for three days before he had had a moment to himself and that was when he remembered he had stood me up. Charming! He said he was so ashamed he couldn't bring himself to contact me. I bet.

His apology was not accepted; I wanted to be left alone so I could concentrate on the good things in my life and I knew Alex was not conducive to my happiness. I was completely through with him.

One Wednesday morning in the second week of September I received an unexpected phone call from my aunt Lily's buyer's advocate friend, Mal. I hadn't given seeing a buyer's advocate a second thought since she had suggested it. I had been focusing on saving, and had put away $41 350, but I wanted to crack the $42 000 mark before I started getting serious again. I still hadn't made an appointment with my bank manager to apply for a loan, and had told myself I would do so once I hit the $42 000 mark. I was still a touch spooked about the idea of having my credit history checked. I also had never received a follow-up call about my loan preliminary pre-approval, so I figured that I'd somehow slipped through the cracks there, which didn't bother me at all! I'd rather leave that embarrassing incident behind.

I chatted with Mal and he told me he thought he might be able to give me a hand, so we organised an informal meeting for the following Saturday.

The night before I was to meet Mal for our morning meeting, I attended a huge 33rd birthday party that was being thrown for Jillian, a girl Eliza and I had gone to high school with. I didn't want to go, but Eliza said I had to come and check out the place Jillian had just bought.

Jillian's apartment was located in one of the trendy western suburbs about 15 minutes from the CBD and across the city's main bridge. The area used to be quite poor, but young working couples had started to move in about 10 years earlier. They had renovated their houses; opened bars, cafés and bookshops; and returned the area to its pre-war glory. As we were driving to the party, I remarked to Eliza that I was certain Jillian's home would be the size of a shoebox. But it wasn't; it was absolutely fantastic.

Jillian was single, and had purchased a two-bedroom, two-level apartment four months earlier on her own. She had only recently moved in. It was a brand-new building on a main road, but quite close to the local café strip. Her apartment had an open-plan living and kitchen area on one floor, looking over a small, but sweet, courtyard. On that floor there was also a bedroom and big central bathroom. It was beautifully decorated and I was green with envy.

However, it wasn't until our tour went upstairs that I was really blown away. Jillian's second level comprised of a huge master bedroom, with a built-in robe and ensuite. She had her very own private sanctuary and she had made it both stylish and comfortable. I could barely keep my mouth off the floor.

When we got back downstairs, Jillian told me she had never thought she would buy an apartment but when she saw this place she had known it was perfect for her. She said she had looked for more than a year and either hated or couldn't afford every house she'd seen. Finally, her sister had convinced her to look at a few apartments and she had found her home.

'I walked in and felt completely at home', she gushed. 'It was brand new, no-one had lived here before and they had gorgeous furniture everywhere for the inspections. I also felt really safe, which wasn't something I'd been concerned about before as a single woman. I knew it was the one for me, but, just to be safe, I got a buyer's advocate to manage the purchase. And voila!'

My hopes were now absolutely buoyed about my meeting the next day with Mal, the buyer's advocate my aunt suggested I talk to.

The next morning I woke up feeling remarkably fresh and excited about meeting Mal to talk property. Mal was not at all what I expected. He was a man in his late 50s, who wore a tweed hat and glasses. He looked like Sherlock Holmes; not anything like most of the people I had encountered in the real estate game so far.

I told him I didn't have any finance yet, but had $41 350 saved and had been told by a financial adviser that I would probably be able to borrow in the region of $370 000. (I left out the part about doing a preliminary pre-approval online.)

'So, what are you trying to achieve?' he asked.

I thought this was a pretty silly question and explained to him that I wanted to buy my own home, of course.

'No, what I mean is, is this a house you are going to live in or rent out? And are you going to live in it forever or sell it in five years? Have you got a plan for the future?'

He was firing questions at me so fast that I needed a moment to get my head around what he saying. 'My plan was to save for the deposit, find a house, get a loan and move in', I said. 'I haven't thought about whether I plan to sell it one or 10 years from now. My priority is to find something I can afford in an area I like.'

Mal said I was a typical first home buyer, which I thought meant I basically had no idea what I was doing.

'Many people start by saying they need to find a house', he said. 'So they go and start looking at houses and then they make a plan to fit that house and work out how they can afford it. What you should be doing is sitting down and working out a plan and *then* looking at houses to see if any of them fit your plan. Does that make sense?'

Mal went on to explain that while buying property could be an emotional experience, it really shouldn't be — I needed to fit my property to my finances, not my finances to the property. He explained that I should be planning not just for what I needed now, but also for the next five years.

'Are you single?' he asked suddenly.

'Yes. Is that a problem?' No wonder not many women bought property on their own if these were the types of questions they came up against! Why should my marital status matter? It should just be about finances!

'Of course it's not a problem. It just means you will have to factor in meeting the right partner or having a child, if that's what you want to do. If these things are a consideration for you, then you want to find a property that gives you flexibility. Do you want to have an option to stay in the house with a child? Or will you want to be able to sell it and upgrade to a bigger house, perhaps with a backyard?'

I was a tad perturbed by the baby talk and I wasn't quite sure of the importance of finding a man, but I put it to the back of my mind and pressed on.

'I don't know what's in my future', I said. 'I'm single, I have no prospects romantically and consequently I have not given much thought to having children. I just want to own some property. At this stage in the game it can be a block of a land with a shed and toilet on it if need be.'

'These are just standard questions. Okay, Maggie, so where have you been looking and what have you found so far?' Mal was clearly ignoring my single woman's lament.

I explained the parameters of my search to him.

'Well, you're on the right track looking in the inner suburbs', he said. 'The inner suburbs will give you emotional and financial options in the future—better resale value and higher rental yield. If the first property you buy is a bad investment and doesn't appreciate enough, the chances are that the second property you upgrade to—say, if you have a baby and want more space—is going to be equally as bad an investment. This is because the people you will be competing with will also be upgrading, and they may have made a better investment the first time around, giving them more money to play with than you.

'If you don't get a good deal with your second property, the chances are that you'll never be able to make up for lost ground and buy your dream house one day—that is, not without some outside help or a Lotto win. What I say to many first home buyers is that if you're in a McMansion in the far-out suburbs after your second property purchase, that's where you are going to end up living forever—all things being equal—as those types of places will never appreciate as much as a good inner suburb.

'Now, what research have you been doing?'

I was a little overwhelmed by what he had just said, but I told him I had been to inspections and auctions almost every Saturday since the beginning of the year and I had daily email updates from the house-hunting website. 'I just don't know if I will ever be able to actually afford a house in the areas I am looking at', I continued. 'Do you think I should be looking for an apartment instead?'

He nodded at me as if I'd asked him a really good question, which made me feel less stupid.

'Well, I would recommend always buying land because, historically, land is what will give you value and growth, and that growth will give you options going forward', he explained. 'If you are dead-set on staying in the inner suburbs and you can't afford a house, I'd suggest you at least go for an old-style nana's unit or a townhouse with a little bit of land attached, as that's better than just an apartment. To tell you the truth, though, you're in a very difficult situation here because you'll be struggling to even find a two-bedroom apartment for $400 000 in the inner suburbs these days.'

Undeterred, I told him about Jillian's new apartment and how luxurious, safe and spacious it was.

The look on his face was as if he'd bitten into a lemon. He proceeded to pull no punches. 'You'd be unwise to buy a brand-new apartment. A new apartment is like a new BMW: as soon as you drive out of the showroom, they lose value and their worth decreases to that of a second-hand one. So if you're going to have to buy an apartment, buy an older one that has room for improvement. But I'd much rather you buy a place with some land.'

I wasn't sure what I wanted at that point in time. I told him I still wasn't 100 per cent sure how much I could borrow, anyway.

'Okay. You don't owe me anything for our chat today', he said. 'But if we were going to work together, what I'd do is take you around to a selection of properties that I think fit your needs—both financially and emotionally—and I would help you work out not only what you want, but also what you need. I charge between $5000 and $7000 for my services, which includes negotiating the sale for you. Is this something you can factor into your budget?'

Seven thousand dollars? I knew he wouldn't be free, but that seemed like a lot of money—a lot of money that I just didn't have! I would have loved to be able to afford Mal's expertise, but that fee was way out of my league.

'Thanks, Mal', I said, getting up from my chair and collecting my things, 'but I think I'm going to have to go this alone. You've been a great help, though, and I appreciate it. I have a lot to think about.'

'Okay. Then my final piece of advice to you is this: before you do anything else, go and see a mortgage broker about getting a home loan.'

A mortgage broker? But I was going to make an appointment to see the bank manager. It looked like I'd have to rethink that, as well. When was I going to get a handle on the whole house-hunting gig? Surely this had to get easier.

Lessons learned

- Beware of the emotional purchase. It's fair to say every house-hunter is going to fall in love with their dream home, but it doesn't mean that it's the right one.

- Don't be afraid to go and talk to your local bank. They will be able to provide you with information about all the ins and outs of getting a mortgage.

- Get a formal pre-approval for a loan before you put in an offer. This way you'll know exactly how much money you have to spend and won't give yourself a hernia stressing about it.

- Don't go out with men who don't call you for weeks at a time, or leave the country without telling you.

- Always wear waterproof mascara.

- Expand your house-hunting horizons. If you are flexible in what you are looking for and where you are looking, you have more of a chance of finding the right place.

- Buyer's advocates can be invaluable if you are able to spare the money to use one. They will not only help you find the right house, but will do the bidding or negotiating for you as well.

PART IV

Coming to terms

October to December

Dream home: anything with a front door
    and a toilet
Savings: $42250
Deposit needed: $40000
Deposit wanted: about $42000—got it!
Happiness: relieved

In the last three weeks of September I had kept up my
intense saving regimen to add almost another $1100 to
my total. There were less than two months until my 33rd
birthday and I was on a mission to find a house by the big
day. I definitely had the 10 per cent deposit for a $400 000
home, plus a little more, and all I needed was pre-approval
for a home loan. The property market was in full swing,
with a record number of houses for sale. The problem
was that they were still going for tens of thousands of
dollars above the advertised prices and I finally had to
accept that my dream of buying a two-bedroom house
in any of the suburbs I had been searching was just that:
a dream.

Mal had said I needed a plan and had recommended
that I go and see a mortgage broker to find out how
much I was going to be able to lend. Rather than just
me going to one bank, a mortgage broker was able to
research and offer me any number of home loans from
various lenders. Within a week of my meeting with Mal,
I had found a reputable national mortgage broking
company that not only had a good reputation but also
did not charge customers for its residential loan services.
I called them and made an appointment. I also made the
long-awaited appointment with my bank manager. I still
wasn't entirely convinced that a big bank would give me a

mortgage but, if things didn't go well with the broker, at least I would have somewhere else to turn straight away.

The mortgage broker's receptionist had put me through to a man called George. He was chatty and sounded like the kind of person who would be more than willing to help me out. I had been nervous making the call, but he immediately put me at ease.

The phone call started off a bit like a date, as he said, 'So, tell me a little bit about yourself, Maggie'.

I had to remind myself that he just wanted to know the facts and figures, not my star sign and favourite movie! 'Well, I'm 32, I earn $65 000 a year and I have saved a little over $42 000. I have no other debts and I want my own home. Will you give me a mortgage?' I asked, sounding more than a little desperate.

George laughed heartily down the line. 'Yeah, I think we should be able to help you out. How much do you want to borrow? Have you found a house to purchase yet?'

I explained that I hadn't found a place yet—I thought it best to leave out the Treasury Street fiasco!—and that I was hoping to get pre-approval to be able to buy a place for about $400 000.

'Well, there are a few things we need to talk about before we get started finding you a lender', he said, far more optimistically than I was feeling. 'First things first: before I meet with you in person, we need to arrange a credit check.'

There it was again: the dreaded credit check. Panic set in as I thought about all those parking fines I had not paid until the very last minute; the credit card repayments I had put off paying for weeks before transferring some money across and then just racking up the credit again the next day; the number of times I had swapped banks to get a low-interest credit card, telling myself I'd pay it off if my repayments were smaller, but still never managing to do so. I knew all this would come back to haunt me, and the day of reckoning had come in the form of a conversation with a kindly mortgage broker.

'Okay, time to confess', I steadied myself. 'Here's the thing. I have been saving diligently for almost three years now but I've been really bad with my money in the past. In fact, I'm really worried that my credit history will be appalling. Is that a big problem?'

George asked me to explain my problems further.

'Well, I had credit card debts up to my eyeballs, I could never pay a bill on time and I had more overdue parking fines to pay for in one year than most people would have in a lifetime.'

But George didn't seem fazed. 'Okay, I'll get a copy of your credit history and see what sort of damage you've done with your parking fines and credit card debts. The credit history is often called your Veda File, after the company that does the checks. Anyone can get a copy of their credit record. It costs about $50 and they will send it to you confidentially.

'Now, a lot of the things you're worried about often don't show up on a credit history—many people worry about their credit history unnecessarily. They think what they've done in the past will be a black mark against them forever, but in reality the debt may not even have been listed.'

The man clearly didn't know who he was dealing with. I had been a super-debt-making machine.

'What types of things *are* actually left as permanent reminders of people's misdemeanours, exactly?' I asked him cagily.

'The things that are listed are usually the ones you don't even know about', he said. 'You will have a mark on your credit record if you have unsettled debts. For example, if you have continued to ignore letters from the council for overdue parking fines and they are forced to use a debt collector, that will show up more often than not on your credit history. Or if you have decided to ignore your bank when they were asking for credit card repayments, that might also come up. So if all your outstanding debts have been paid, your credit check should be okay. But if the debts were ever unsettled or left unsettled for a long period of time, it will be a lot harder for us to get you a loan. It also depends on how many times you have accessed extra credit and things like that. The credit check is a really major component of getting a mortgage.'

I explained to George that I hadn't used a credit card in years because of the damage I did last time. And I was pretty sure I currently had no outstanding bills — at least, there was nothing I could think of. I just hoped that the amount of time I'd taken to eventually clear my debts wouldn't be my downfall.

'Maggie, a period of three years debt-free, with no outstanding debts, is pretty good. If it were yesterday or a year ago that you had started saving, then it could be a problem, but the banks will take you on your current merit. They will look at your savings history; whether it's been consistent and whether you have shown responsible behaviour. Being able to indicate a track record of responsible behaviour is the key thing here. And if there are any problems, we'll get you onto a law firm we use that fixes credit.'

Fix credit! Things were finally looking up for me. 'What do you mean by "fix credit"?' I asked.

'We actually use a law firm that takes credit files and "cleans" them. It's really great, although it costs about $1500. Basically they take the fines to court and fight them — especially old parking fines, which some councils are diligent at registering on credit files if left unpaid. It's quite amazing what a good lawyer can do, though.

'The other good news about credit histories is that they are recorded in rolling five-year blocks, so if you had a default on your card from four years and 364 days ago, but you had paid it, tomorrow it would vanish from the record.'

That was good and well for people who had issues five years ago, but mine were a little closer than that. The last time I had had problems paying off debts was only three years earlier. I vividly remembered opening a legal letter that said I only had a week to pay several hundred dollars in fines that I had completely ignored. It wasn't the first time, either. I'd once been sent a solicitor's letter from a video store demanding I pay the fine on an overdue crappy Richard Gere film. I was mortified when I had to show Eliza the letter to make sure I wasn't going to face court. And to add insult to injury, she then went and stuck it up on our toilet door when I lived with her, to remind me of what happens when you don't pay fines.

George continued to reassure me that we definitely had options now that I was on the straight and narrow with my debt and savings.

'Okay', I said. 'If I was able to get a mortgage, how much do you think I would be able to borrow?' The only thing I'd really wanted to know throughout the whole conversation was if I had any chance of being approved for a loan.

'I'll do an over-the-phone qualifier now to see who you might be able to get a home loan from and how much you could borrow. It's not a definitive yes; it just gives us a guide for when we meet and we have the results of your credit history. Once I've done the credit check and we've sorted out any issues, we can approach those different lenders to try to get you a mortgage.'

George ran some numbers and, on the basis of my current income and savings, the fact that I have no known debts, my marital status (single) and number of dependents (zero), he said there were a few lenders who would probably be willing to give me a mortgage.

'Based on your financial details, we could probably get you a loan amount of about $380 000 — and you'd need at least that to purchase a $400 000 house because, although you have a lot of money saved, you probably know that you'll need to pay a lot of fees on top of the price of the property. I should tell you, though, that with a loan of that size your mortgage repayments will be fairly steep. On an income of $65 000, your monthly budget would need to be pretty tight, and you wouldn't have much cash left over each month to splash around.'

It was the story of my life!

'Do you have a preference of money lender?' he continued. 'Do you want to stick with one of the major players? Looking at the figures in front of me, your current options are Rock Lenders, Star Building Society and Sunnyside Loans, which is affiliated with Universal Bank. It looks like Sunnyside has the lowest interest rate.'

'What would you recommend?'

'I'm going to be honest with you. In your situation, you are not going to have a lot of options. You don't have a lot of money and you have no collateral. That is, you don't own anything; you have no assets. Star Building Society and Rock Lenders are offering less money with higher interests rates.

'Sunnyside loans is offering the best deal here. The loan has a cheap interest rate and no ongoing fees. It offers free redraw, which means that if you have made extra repayments to your home loan or have paid off more each month than you are expected to pay, you will be "ahead" in your payments and you can draw that extra money out of your loan account when or if you need it.

'It also offers a free offset facility. An offset account is basically a savings account linked to your loan account, and the savings in that account can be "offset" against the principal amount owing on your loan, to help you pay off the loan more quickly.

'These are not things you will want to do immediately, but it's good to have those options in the future. This loan also has no exit fees, so you won't be penalised if you decide to change to a different lender later on.'

'I already have a savings account with Universal so it makes sense to go with Sunnyside if they are offering the best deal.'

At that point I would have taken the money from my grandmother.

George and I arranged a time to meet up in person later in the week and, less than 30 minutes after I got off the phone, he sent me a follow-up email and the details of the home loan qualifier we had discussed.

From: George Leonard
Sent: Monday, 3 October 10:14 AM
To: Maggie Rose
Subject: Home loan

Attachment: Rose qualifier.pdf, enquiryform.doc, customercharter.doc

Hi Maggie

Thanks for your enquiry today. I believe we have a great chance of securing a mortgage for you. As discussed, there is a great lender that will most likely lend you the $380 000 — Sunnyside Home Loans, an arm of the Universal Bank.

I have attached a qualifier from Sunnyside showing the breakdown of costs and, more importantly, the mortgage repayments. We can go through the details of this when we meet. You need to fill out the attached enquiry form, which details your personal and financial history.

I have also attached my customer charter, which explains how I do my business.

When we meet, I will have done a credit check for you, which we can go through. If you're happy to proceed after that, a pre-approval can be entered into the system.

I will also need you to bring the following documents to our meeting:

- Your last two pay slips
- Copies of your drivers licence and passport
- Statements from the last 90 days on your savings account
- Your completed enquiry form (see attached)

I look forward to seeing you at the end of the week.

Regards,
George Leonard | Mortgage Broker

I phoned the local bank and cancelled my meeting with the bank manager. I was going to stick with George. I had a good feeling about him. I wouldn't say my gut instinct never led me astray (let's face it!), but this time I felt as though I was onto a winner.

While it had been really reassuring to talk with an expert, I still had a niggling feeling something could go wrong. Even though I had been sure I had no outstanding debts, in the hours after our conversation I became convinced that I had a rogue parking fine somewhere that I had never paid. There had been so many—I now had no doubt that one would have slipped through the cracks to trip me up. I'd moved house three times in five years, so there was a good chance that a letter had been sent to an address where I no longer resided. I hadn't had a car for two years, but before that every council in the city would have been aware that I existed, just because of the huge number of late letters sent to me. But I needed to accept that there was nothing I could do about it; it was out of my hands and I wouldn't know anything until George did the credit check.

Isobel called me that afternoon to invite me back onto *The Real Nightly News* that week. It had been a few weeks since I'd been on the show, and I was looking forward to it. Getting the invitation knocked me out of my reverie and made me realise that my career seemed to be going really well; that things in my life could have been worse. And it wasn't the end of the world if I couldn't get a home loan. If I couldn't borrow money for a house, I could just rent somewhere really lovely on my own again. Or I could learn how to invest. I had $42 000, for pete's sake! Dabbling in shares wasn't something I'd given a lot of thought to, but the sharemarket was recovering from the credit crisis and I was sure Jason, my financial adviser, would be able to tell me where my money would best be spent if it wasn't going into property. People made millions buying and selling shares; there was no reason I couldn't do the same.

'Maggie Rose', I said to myself, 'you have options'.

When I arrived at the radio station for my weekly spot that Thursday morning, Angelica wasn't there. It was the first time she hadn't been there in the nine months I had been working at the radio. It didn't matter where she was; the point was she wasn't at work to stare at me and make me feel uncomfortable. It was sweet relief after so much torment. I was no longer scared of her since I had seen her drunk at the Metro party, but seeing her each week had started to hurt more, for reasons that I couldn't quite put my finger on.

'Where's Angelica?' I asked the producer who was filling in.

'She's on holidays for a few weeks. I think she's in Paris or somewhere.'

The happiness drained from by body. The thought of Spencer and Angelica together in Paris was sickening. I did my radio spot and chatted away about meeting George the mortgage broker and explained to listeners the information he'd given me about credit histories, but I couldn't stop thinking about Spencer and Angelica frolicking along the Seine eating baguettes with stinky cheese.

That afternoon, however, the best news I'd had in years arrived in my inbox to cheer me up.

From: George Leonard
Sent: Thursday, 6 October 4:32 PM
To: Maggie Rose
Subject: Credit check

Attachment: enquiryform.doc

To Maggie

I have some good news: your credit check was okay.

See you tomorrow morning at 8 am, and remember to bring the following:

- Your last two pay slips
- Copies of your drivers licence and passport
- Statements from the last 90 days on your savings account
- Your completed enquiry form (attached again)

Regards,
George Leonard | Mortgage Broker

I had to read the email five times before it completely sunk in. I had passed the credit check and there were no skeletons in my closet stopping me from applying for a home loan! I didn't know what to do with myself. I sat at my desk staring at the email, but what I really wanted to do was run around the office and kiss all my colleagues—at that stage I would have even kissed the evil Janice!

I emailed Genevieve and told her we were going out for a quick celebration after work; no arguments. As soon as the clock struck five, we ran out of the office for a very quick glass of champagne before I had to catch a taxi over to Metro for that night's TV show.

'So, what happens next?' Genevieve asked.

'I'm not 100 per cent sure, but I'm seeing the mortgage broker tomorrow to discuss pre-approval. You know what, though? Let's not talk about me right now. How the hell are you? How's the man?'

Despite sitting within metres of each other in the office, Genevieve and I barely saw each other at work anymore. She had been made the part-time night chief of staff and was only in the office for two day shifts a week—the other three days she started work at 5 pm. It had been weeks since we'd had a good chat and, while I was totally excited about my home loan news, I finally felt as though a weight had been lifted off my shoulders. I could think clearly enough again to focus on other things; in this case the old flame Genevieve had rekindled while she'd been home in Scotland recently!

'I feel so out of the loop', I said when she told me they were still going strong. 'Are you missing him desperately with you being here and him still being in Scotland?'

'I want to spend the rest of my life with him', she gushed. 'You know how everyone says you know when The One comes along? Well, that's how I feel about Mac and he feels that way about me, too. We miss each other so much that he's coming to Australia in six weeks.'

'For good?'

'Hopefully.'

I couldn't help smiling. I had never heard Genevieve gush. She had been in Australia for a long time and had never met anyone she truly felt a connection with. Aside from my relationship with Spencer, all my other relationships during my 20s and early 30s had been very short-lived, and I'd spent much of my time single. Genevieve and I had spent a lot of mad nights out on the tare, trying to meet decent men, but 99 per cent of the time we'd gone home alone.

'I'm so happy for you, darling', I said to Genevieve. 'You deserve this.' And I meant it, too.

Since we were on a time limit before I rushed off to the TV studio, I only had time to give Genevieve a brief update on the rest of my news. She was especially curious about Alex's disappearing act and his extraordinarily lame 'forgetting' to contact me. We both decided that there must have been more to it than he was telling me.

'Now that I'm not with Alex, I can see how weird it was that every time he'd go away to work he wouldn't call me or allow me to call him', I said. 'His phone was always off. I guess I just wanted to ignore it. And I liked the company, although that sounds a bit pathetic. He did have his moments—when he wasn't being a prat!—but the truth is that I just haven't been that torn up about his departure.'

Genevieve was quick to dismiss him. 'Well, just forget him. He's not worth it and I'm sure the truth will reveal itself in time. It always does! What about Angelica? Is she still giving you grief?'

'No, she's in Paris with Spencer', I said as I gulped down the last of my drink. 'Sometimes I wish I'd never met either of them!'

Genevieve gave me a sideways look and raised her eyebrow. 'Are you telling me that if Spencer was single, you wouldn't be even a tiny bit happy?'

I pushed my chair back from the table and stood to leave. 'I don't know', I sighed. 'If my relationship with Spencer was meant to be, it shouldn't have been that hard for us to stay together. I do wish we could be good friends, but I don't think that's possible while he's with that madwoman. Out of the ex-boyfriends I have, Spencer's the only one I would still like to have in my life. I don't really know what that means.'

I had seen Isobel at the TV station since my debut-night wrap party, but I hadn't had a chance to properly catch up with her to find out what had happened between her and Benjamin at the party. I was pretty sure that if something exciting had happened she would have let me know. My matchmaking skills had never been good at the best of times, so I wasn't surprised that I'd failed at setting up two people I barely knew.

Arriving at the Metro studios that night, I had hoped to catch Isobel for a quick coffee before I was due in for the pre-show briefing, but she wasn't in her office. I saw Madeleine in the corridor and she told me Isobel was at an appointment and would be in at 7 pm. I wondered who was going to take me through my paces before the show if neither Spencer nor Isobel were there. I walked down the unusually empty corridor and found Benjamin.

'Maggie, great to see you', Benjamin said.

'Where is everybody?' I asked him. 'This place is usually buzzing.'

'There are a couple of people on annual leave and I think Isobel is coming in late. I've got a meeting now. You should come and have a drink with a few of us after the show tonight. No wrap party; we're just going across to Leighton to the pub.'

I told Benjamin I'd think about it and went down to the cafeteria to get a takeaway coffee before heading back to the offices to find out who was going to brief me. When I reached Isobel's office again, I did a double-take. Spencer was sitting in one of Isobel's guest chairs. Why was Spencer there? Did Angelica go to Paris without him?

He looked up and smiled, but I must have looked shocked to see him, because he immediately asked me if I was okay. I wasn't prepared to ask him any questions, though, so I told him I was fine, fumbled through a greeting and sat down on the other guest chair, my mind racing the whole time.

He took me through the agenda for that night, but I couldn't concentrate. All I could do was wonder why he was sitting across from me when Angelica was in Paris! I had started entertaining the idea that he and Angelica had broken up, and it was making me giddy. Genevieve's question about my feelings for Spencer had been right on the money—just a hint that there might be trouble in his and Angelica's paradise was all it took for me to start having visions of me instead of Angelica with Spencer, walking hand in hand along the Champs Élysées.

'Are you sure you're okay, Maggie?' Spencer's voice jolted me out of my daydream. 'You still look a little … mystified.' I realised that Spencer had finished his brief, and I had not heard a word of it.

I nodded hazily. 'Oh, yeah, sure. Got it all. No problem', I said, a little too enthusiastically.

'Okay, then. You can head off to wardrobe and make-up.' He didn't look too convinced.

Isobel came and found me while I was having my make-up done. I wanted to get the goss on Spencer and Angelica, but asked her about Benjamin and the wrap party first.

'I went home', she said. 'Alone. I could see you speaking to Spencer at the bar and I didn't want to disturb you, so I just left. Benjamin was acting really weirdly and I wanted to get into bed and put my head under the covers to recover from our night out the night before. I have been meaning to call you but my mum's been sick and I've been so busy helping out with caring for her.'

I felt doubly terrible now that *I* hadn't called *her.* I sympathised with Isobel as she told me about her mum's illness, and made sure she knew she had my support. She then told me what had happened with Benjamin.

'After you left us alone, Spencer's girlfriend came over and started cracking private jokes with Benjamin that I wasn't a part of. I guess she and Benjamin know each other pretty well. She was really drunk, but Benjamin just stood there laughing with her and I felt so stupid. It was awful—I felt like a fifth wheel and I knew I wouldn't get anywhere with him. Everything's been strictly professional with us since then, although...' She smiled coyly.

'Yeah?'

'Well, just after I arrived he came to my office and asked if I wanted to go and have a drink tonight in Leighton. But it's not a date. He said you're coming, too. And it sounded as though he'd invited other people as well. But it'll be nice to see him outside of work again; and probably good to have others around to help me relax. I still really like him and get so nervous around him.'

I promised Isobel that I would definitely go to the drinks that night and be her wing-woman, before Madeleine pulled out the blow-dryer to start doing my hair. Usually she put my hair up, but this time she decided to do a big, bouncy blow-wave. Something I hadn't done myself for months; not since I'd started seeing Alex. She finished off the look with a coat of red lipstick. I felt like Claudia Schiffer; just a tad more buxom.

I was then quickly whisked through wardrobe and into a simple blue shirt dress. Before I had had time to really gauge how I looked in the ensemble, lipstick and all, I was on air.

My 15 minutes on air went by in a flash and I did it without making a single mistake — amazing, as I hadn't absorbed a word of Spencer's briefing. When I was finished, I put my own clothes back on and went to find Isobel. I was surprised to find Isobel having her hair and make-up done, and I was suddenly glad to have not wiped off my own make-up so that I didn't look so frumpy next to her.

'One of the few perks of the job: getting my hair and make-up done before a night out!' Isobel laughed as Madeleine finished straightening her hair.

We caught a taxi together to the pub, and were the first people from the show to arrive. I could see that Isobel was getting nervous, and as I bought her a drink I tried to reassure her that other people — and I — would be there to make things easier. We found a table and waited for Benjamin and the others. Five minutes later, Benjamin and Spencer walked in and indicated that they were going to get a drink before they sat down with us.

'I wonder where everyone else is?' Isobel said, suddenly really concerned that the party would be too small for her to handle. 'I didn't know Spencer was coming, Maggie. Are you alright with this?'

'It's fine', I lied, as my pulse went into overdrive. 'We're friends. It's fine. He's fine. I'm fine. We'll be fine. Just fine.'

Isobel gave me a weird look as Benjamin and Spencer sat down with their drinks; Spencer opposite me and Benjamin opposite Isobel. It was just a tad awkward. Isobel and Benjamin could barely look at one another. I felt, and no doubt looked, uncomfortable, but Spencer was cool as a cucumber.

'Really good show tonight, Maggie and Benjamin. It was hilarious', Spencer said, taking a sip of his drink.

Benjamin didn't seem to have heard Spencer. He and Isobel were both looking around, everywhere but at each other, and I felt a duty to Isobel to act relaxed.

'Yeah it *was* brilliant', I enthused. 'Benjamin, I almost cracked up when you asked the police minister why he had given the go-ahead for a $10 000 speed camera on a dead-end country road rather than on the busiest intersection in the city. He looked like he wanted to kill you.'

'Yeah, I was in the green room cringing', Isobel finally joined the conversation. 'It was so tense I could barely watch.'

The first drinks went down quickly and I could see Benjamin and Isobel relaxing as the conversation picked up. The longer the four of us sat there talking, the clearer it was that Spencer was there to help out Benjamin with Isobel. He was providing a steady stream of drinks and was talking up Benjamin to Isobel whenever there was a second of silence.

Soon Isobel and Benjamin were chatting enthusiastically with each other, and I realised that Spencer and I were sitting self-consciously on our end of the table, not talking. I looked up from my drink and awkwardly caught his eye.

'So…' he said.

'So…' I said, smiling.

'So, have you bought a house yet?'

The silence was broken and I launched into the good news about passing my credit check and how nervous I'd been. There was something about talking to Spencer when I wasn't at his work or at an auction that made me feel at ease. It was familiar and comfortable. Before long, we started to talk about the old days and he was asking me how Eliza, Max and Jem were going.

'Remember that night when I knocked on your front door before you went away for Max and Jem's wedding?' Spencer reminisced.

Did I remember? It was one of the best nights of my life. Spencer and I had had a huge misunderstanding and had stopped talking to each other. It was early days in our relationship and I was miserable at the thought that I'd ruined everything. Eliza had contacted Spencer and made him come over and make up with me. She told me later that she had intervened because she wouldn't go to Malaysia with me for the wedding if I was going to mope for a week.

'Yeah, Eliza was a maniac', I joked. But really I was daydreaming about how Spencer and I had made up, and how beautiful our relationship had been after that—at least, until he left for Japan.

Spencer and I decided to sneak off to the bar together to get a round of drinks and leave Isobel and Benjamin alone for a while. They seemed to be hitting it off and didn't seem to mind if we were there or not. I couldn't help asking Spencer why Benjamin had acted like such an idiot around Isobel the last time we'd all been out together.

Spencer immediately leapt to his defence. 'He's very shy and he was really drunk. He told me what happened and it's taken me this long to convince him to ask Isobel out. But he would only do it on the proviso that you and I came along for support.'

Ah, that's why no-one else had turned up.

Spencer looked me in the eye and smiled. 'Of course, I was happy to oblige.'

It was that cheeky smile of his that made me go weak at the knees. What was he doing, giving me *that* smile? And why hadn't he mentioned Angelica once in the entire time we'd been talking? I felt as though he was playing with my emotions—it just wasn't fair. I grabbed two of the drinks and turned on my heel, away from his smile. I made a beeline back over to the table, leaving Spencer at the bar to pay for the drinks.

I got back to the table to find that Isobel had gone to the toilets and left Benjamin alone. Benjamin looked ecstatic.

'You look like you're having a good night', I smiled at Benjamin, trying to push thoughts of Spencer to the back of my mind for a moment.

'Thanks for agreeing to come along tonight, Maggie, especially after I was such a moron last time. I really am sorry about that—I was drunk and it was easier to have a laugh with Angelica than try to talk to Isobel. And I didn't realise that you and Spencer have history too, so I doubly appreciate you coming along tonight after I had been fraternising with Angelica—the enemy.'

'She's not my enemy', I said defensively. 'I don't really know her.'

'I've actually gotten to know her a bit this year through Spencer, and she's pretty good value. But I'm not sure her and Spencer are a good match.'

It was as though he'd read my thoughts—only moments earlier I had been thinking about whether Spencer gave his knee-weakening smile to Angelica and if it made her go weak at the knees, too…or if she was so hardened that she was impenetrable to his charm. I looked up sharply and Benjamin was giving me a knowing smile. I must have been a dead giveaway. I finally had to admit to myself that I was not over Spencer. And that maybe it had been obvious to everyone but me.

Isobel and Spencer were both heading back to the table, and I decided that it was time for me to leave. If I was so transparent to Benjamin, who didn't even know me, then what did Spencer and Isobel see? I stood up and grabbed my handbag, saying my goodbyes. Spencer suddenly said he was leaving, too. 'I'll get you a taxi out the front.'

I didn't want to be around Spencer anymore, but Isobel looked pleased that we were both leaving, and I owed her. I begrudgingly walked outside with him.

There wasn't a taxi in sight. I called the taxi company and was told that my booking would take at least half an hour. Why was the universe tormenting me like this? Why was I repeatedly being thrown into these situations with Spencer?

'I'm going to start walking', I said to Spencer.

'I will too, then.'

Great—I just couldn't win. Why couldn't he leave me alone?

We started walking along the street and I did my best to act as though there wasn't a big white elephant between us. We were barely a few steps from the pub when Spencer suddenly stopped and turned to me. 'Maggie', he said.

Oh, no. He was going to tell me that he could see I was still in love with him and give me the 'just friends' talk. This was going to be so humiliating.

I slowly turned to face him.

'Maggie', he began, 'I just want to say I'm really happy that we're able to work together as friends'.

Yep, there it was—how was I going to lie my way out of this one? *Yeah, I'm really happy to be tormented by seeing you and your girlfriend every week at work, too.*

But before I had a chance to reply, he continued, 'And I'm sorry for acting weird this year. It's been hard to see you.'

Huh? It had been hard for him? But he'd been as cool as a cucumber—I'd been the one making a fool out of myself, acting weirdly and thinking jealous thoughts.

I didn't reply; I was too surprised. I just stood staring blankly at him.

'Maggie,' Spencer said stepping towards me, 'I really miss you'.

Before I knew it, I had blurted out, 'I miss you, too'.

Spencer smiled and pulled me into a hug. My head was pressed against his chest and I didn't want to let go. It felt so good to be back in his embrace again. And he smelled just the way I remembered. I breathed deeply and sunk into his chest.

'Maggie', Spencer said again. I looked up from where I was snuggled into his jacket. His big eyes were looking down at me intently and I was lost for a second in his gaze. My trance was broken as his hand gently cupped my chin; he lifted my face towards his as he leaned down to kiss me.

The kiss lasted only a few seconds, but for me it was like an explosion had gone off. I stumbled backwards, away from Spencer, my head spinning. What did this mean? What was going on? Why would he do this? Does he still love me? Would we get back together? But as my thoughts began to slow down, one big factor quickly dawned on me. Angelica. I needed to get the hell out of there.

Obviously that kiss had meant nothing to Spencer. How could it? It was probably just a pity kiss because I looked so desperate and had held him so tightly. Spencer had Angelica. I had no-one. Tears sprung to my eyes and my lips, which had so recently been pressed against Spencer's, began to tremble. Why had I become such a blubbering mess? I knew why. It was because I found the idea of Spencer and Angelica together so repulsive that it had actually made me cry. That must have been it.

I looked dartingly about—I needed to get away from Spencer. I wanted to run, but where would I go?

I heard Spencer say my name and noticed that he had taken a step towards me, but just at that second a taxi came hurtling around the corner. I stumbled out onto the road with my arms above my head, daring the taxi not to stop. It screeched to a halt and I ran around to the open window. 'Taxi for Maggie?' the driver said.

Finally, the universe was giving me a break. I got in the taxi without looking back and ordered the driver to go— fast—as the floods of tears finally spilled from my eyes.

I woke groggily the next morning, bleary-headed from having cried myself to sleep the night before. I wanted to stay in bed, but I had a meeting with the mortgage broker before work. I gave myself a pep talk as I got up and got ready. 'Okay, Maggie. Brush yourself off and get on with your life. Spencer will not get the better of you.'

I needed to focus on going to see George and getting the home loan approval. I wasn't going to think about Spencer kissing me. It would drive me crazy.

George worked from home, and when I arrived I found his daughters running around the front yard before school. One of them pointed me in the direction of an office attached to the side of the house, and I went in to find George dressed casually in shorts and a t-shirt. He was in his mid-40s, with sandy blond hair and a tan. He looked like he was about to go surfing. In fact, there were several surfboards lined up outside his office door. Yet despite his casual attire, he was all business.

'You must be Maggie', he greeted me. 'I have good news. With your credit history given the okay, we should definitely be able to get you pre-approval for a home loan.' He had the qualifying sheet from Sunnyside Loans in front of him, which he'd emailed me earlier in the week.

Sunnyside Loans

Client   **Miss Maggie Rose**

Home Loan Consultant   **George Leonard**

Funds Requirement Summary

PURCHASE 1 Owner Occupied New Purchase	
Purchase Price House/Land	$400 000
Borrower Legal Fees	$1000
Lender Application Fees	$600
Property Stamp Duty	$17 476
Mortgage Insurance	$9824
Other	$100
Customer Contribution	$49 000
Funds Required	$380 000
TOTALS	
Total Loan Security Offered	$400 000
LVR	95.00%
Total Customer Contributions	$49 000
Total Loan Amount	$380 000

Loans Summary

LOAN 1 (Purchaser)	
Premium Home Loan	
Product Type	Standard Variable
Interest	Variable
Amortisation	Principal & Interest
Loan Amount	$380 000
Loan Term	30 Years
Standard Rate	6.90%
Repayment Frequency	Monthly
Weekly and fortnightly repayments are true repayments.	
Lender may use different repayment method to calculate.	
Normal Repayment	$2503
Quoted repayment excludes any loan service fee the	
lender may apply. This may differ to figure used in	
loan offer.	

Income Summary

APPLICANT 1 Maggie Rose	
Primary Full-Time Salary/Wages (monthly)	$5417
TOTAL TAXABLE INCOME (monthly)	$5417
TOTAL NON-TAXABLE INCOME (monthly)	$0

Expense Summary

APPLICANT 1 Maggie Rose	
TOTAL EXPENSES (monthly)	$0

The qualifier gave the rundown of all the costs involved and the amount of the repayments I'd have to make. We looked it over together.

'Before we put this through for final approval', George said, 'there are few things the bank is going to want to know. Sunnyside is going to be looking at four main things when they decide whether to give you a home loan: how long you have been in your job; your monthly uncommitted income; the loan-to-value ratio (which is listed on the qualifier), and how long you have lived in your current residence. The banks really love stability of residence, so if you've moved around a lot and lived in, say, 15 different places in the last few years, they're not going to like it'.

I explained to George again that I had moved three times in five years, but had been at my current address for most of the year; before that I had rented an apartment for two years. And I'd been at my current job for close to seven years. All of that shouldn't have posed any problems. I had to ask him, though, to explain what the loan-to-value ratio and the uncommitted monthly income were.

'The loan-to-value ratio, or—as you can see it written on the qualifying sheet—the LVR, is the ratio of the amount you've been loaned to the value of the property. In this instance, you can see it's 95 per cent. Banks usually like this to be as low as possible, but they will often approve a loan with a high LVR. It just means they might charge the borrower more for mortgage insurance because essentially the risk to the bank is greater. You can see that the mortgage insurance in this case is rather expensive.'

This was what my financial adviser, Jason, had been referring to way back in April, when he'd talked of the loan as a percentage of the purchase price. I hadn't understood it then, but it was suddenly making sense. Although Jason had said that I should try to ensure that my loan had a LVR of less than 90 per cent, it would mean sacrificing the apartment I wanted, in the suburb where I wanted to live. But I needed that 95 per cent loan—I would just have to wear the extra insurance costs. Didn't everyone overstretch themselves these days?

'The uncommitted monthly income, or UMI, doesn't appear on the qualifier. It refers to how much money you have left over once you've paid your mortgage each month, and after living expenses. That's really important, too.'

I asked for a sheet of paper and scribbled down some numbers as he spoke.

$65 000 per year = $5417 per month
less tax = $4304
less mortgage ($2503) = $1801
$1801 per month = $415 per week

'You earn $5417 a month', he said, 'and after tax you take home $4304. Sunnyside's standard variable home loan, with 6.9 per cent interest, would see you paying $2503 a month to the bank. So, you would have $1801 per month left over for everything else. The monthly repayment amount seems high, but I can tell you that it's a really good deal. Most of the big banks' interest rates are edging towards 7.9 per cent. Sunnyside is a good option for someone like you who doesn't have a lot of cash to splash around.

'See that number at the bottom there?' He pointed to the $415 written at the bottom of the paper. 'That's what you'll have to live on each week, and it's going to be a tight squeeze.'

So this was the true price of owning my own home. I would have $415 each week to pay all of my bills and also pay for food and entertainment, as well as try to save some extra cash. I could forget about buying new clothes or furniture on that budget.

George could see that the colour had drained from my face. 'You could think about getting someone to rent out a room', he suggested. 'Because you're borrowing to capacity, having a tenant will free up some of your money. Whether or not you have a tenant won't make any difference to the bank, as they'll approve you for a loan based on what you, on your own, can afford. But having a tenant would help you pay the mortgage and leave you with more money to play with. It's something to consider.'

It was true that having a tenant was not something I'd ever considered. But it was definitely a possibility.

George and I then went through the costs listed on the qualifier, and I wrote more notes as we went, to help me understand it clearly.

'After you add the legal fees, stamp duty, mortgage insurance, lender application fees and a small contingency, a $400 000 property will cost you $429 000 all up.'

Property purchase price = $400 000
Associated fees/charges = $29 000
Total to buy property = $429 000

'You will have the $7000 first home owner grant, plus the deposit you've been saving. You told me that you had $42 425 now — is that correct?'

'Yes.'

Property purchase price =	$400 000
Associated fees/charges =	$29 000
Total to buy property =	$429 000

First home owner grant =	$7000
Maggie's savings =	$42 425
Total of Maggie's funds =	$49 425

'Now, with a loan of $380 000, plus your current savings and the grant, you have $429 425. This is great, and covers the funds you need to buy a $400 000 property.'

Property purchase price =	$400 000
Associated fees/charges =	$29 000
Total to buy property =	$429 000

First home owner grant =	$7000
Maggie's savings =	$42 425
Total of Maggie's funds =	$49 425

Loan amount =	$380 000
Maggie's funds =	$49 425
Total Maggie has to spend =	$429 425

'It's great that I have the money to get the mortgage, but what about having a buffer?' I asked.

I clearly remembered Jason talking about having a $5000 buffer for increased mortgage repayments due to increased interest rates, repairs and anything else that cropped up. And I wanted a buffer to buy new furniture!

'You know how I said you'd still be saving? Well, all you need to do is keep saving. By the time you find a house, purchase it and then have the settlement period, you would have saved a lot more if you keep on the track you're on. You'd have an extra few thousand dollars, at least', George assured me. 'Remember that on any property you buy there will be a settlement period of 30 to 90 days, from the time you actually purchase a property to the time it gets handed over to you. It's up to you whether you choose a settlement period of 30, 45, 60 or 90 days, just as long as there is enough time for anything that goes wrong to be fixed! In my experience, once people purchase a property for the first time they are vigilant about putting money away in the weeks leading up to the settlement date. You'll be fine.'

I hadn't thought about the fact that it wouldn't be an immediate settlement; it hadn't occurred to me that I wouldn't just sign a contract to buy a house and have the keys the very next day. I was such an 'instant gratification' kind of gal that the idea of waiting 30 to 90 days would normally have driven me crazy—I couldn't even keep an item on lay-by for a week. But in this case George was right; the settlement period would just give me more time to save for my buffer.

Feeling elated (despite the meagre amount of money I'd have to live on with such a big home loan), I handed over my payslips, copies of my licence and passport, my bank statement and the completed enquiry form. George told me he'd get started with the proper pre-approval application straight away.

'Now remember, the pre-approval will be subject to the lender getting the property valued when you find a house to buy. But essentially it will give you the green light to go ahead and actually make an offer or a bid on property. I'll give you a call once you're pre-approved.

'The next step is for you to find a place, put in an offer and have it accepted! Then you let me know and I tell the bank. The bank will value the property and submit your details for the insurance lender to assess, and you should be good to go.'

I was overwhelmed. This property buying thing was like a roller-coaster ride: I kept fluctuating between excitement and stress.

When I got into the office later that morning, I had the usual barrage of emails from Janice, but there was also an email waiting for me from Spencer.

From: Spencer Lee
Sent: Friday, 7 October 9:02 AM
To: Maggie Rose
Subject:

Hi Maggie,

I'm really sorry about last night. I didn't mean for any of it to happen.

I hope you got home safely.

Spencer

When I closed my eyes I could imagine the feeling of his arms wrapped comfortably around me, hearing his heart beat as I leaned against his chest, his lips pressing against mine... but this email confirmed what I already knew; that it had been a huge mistake on his behalf. As the day was now officially ruined, and my morning elation diminished, I took a deep breath, pressed delete on Spencer's email and started replying to Janice's demands.

Isobel sent me an SMS later that day to tell me that she and Benjamin had kissed the night before, and now they were going on a date. At least someone was kissing and not regretting it.

I had read an article earlier in the week by the property editor, explaining that the month to come was the busiest month of the year for the property market. As I was resolved to buy a house before I turned 33, I had decided once again to ask my dad to accompany me on that Saturday's round of auctions and inspections so we could do some serious house-hunting.

Dad picked me up at 8 am—far too early to be functional on a Saturday morning! There were a few small houses for sale on the outskirts of Surry Hills—a leafy suburb 20 kilometres from the CBD—and we needed time to get there. The houses were all advertised at between $400000 and $500000, but they were a fair way out of town and looked quite rundown. Dad had also pencilled in viewing three apartments in the inner suburb of Kingsley. I hadn't considered looking there, and hadn't looked at apartments before, either. But I was pretty much willing to give anything a go by now, and Dad was being lovely by helping me out, so the least I could do was humour him.

We whizzed through the house inspections in Surry Hills—none of them were what I was looking for—and then drove the 20 kilometres back into town. Both apartments were located on the main boulevard heading into the city. I looked them up on my smartphone as we drove.

The advertisement for the first property said, 'New York loft-style apartment'. Since it was Grace and her husband's amazing New York apartment that had started me on the whole house-hunting adventure to begin with, it was only natural that I should see this place. And it was advertised at between $380 000 and $440 000.

I read the ad out to Dad.

'Stunning modern loft apartment. Two-storey with two bedrooms. Only minutes from the CBD and the bay. Modern kitchen, open living area and a brand-new bathroom. Currently being let for $2009 per calendar month.'

'The rental income is interesting. I know you don't have a car', he said, 'but is there a car space? This apartment is virtually in the middle of the city. There is nowhere to park around here. You are probably going to get a car at some point. And even if you don't, a car space would be desirable if you rent the other room'.

He had a pretty good point, as by then we were doing our second lap of the block trying to find a space to park.

'How do you know so much about this, Dad?' I asked.

'I've been doing some research to help you out. Your mum and I thought you might eventually start looking at apartments.'

We finally found a park and walked a few blocks to the building. It was a mid-1990s building—not what *I* would call 'modern'. Unlike Grace's stunning foyer, the foyer of this building had a worn-out couch and a tired-looking fern in the corner. Dad and I went up to the 15th floor, where we were greeted by an agent—fortunately, one I hadn't dealt with before.

The apartment wasn't quite New York style. It was a small place for two people and I wanted out as soon as I'd walked in.

'This is so frustrating', I told Dad as we walked down the road to the next inspection.

'It is. But you'll find the right place eventually. It's all trial and error with house-hunting. Especially if you don't have a lot of money.'

The next place was 500 metres down the road in a brand-new building. It was also a two-bedroom place, but this one had a car space. It was gorgeous and I was sure it was going to sell for the upper end of the $400 000 to $460 000 price range.

The foyer was unbelievable. It was a glass atrium with big club lounges and massive indoor plants. The apartment was on the 8th floor and everything about it was impeccable. The bedrooms were spacious, with floor to ceiling robes. The bathroom was luxurious, while the kitchen was warm and inviting and had all the mod cons. There was also a small balcony with views looking out over the bay. I could totally see myself living there.

On the way home I was talking to Dad about the place as though I already owned it.

'You need to relax', he countered. 'You've only seen two apartments and they were in an area you've never shown any interest in living before. Also, the apartment you say you love is brand new. Remember how Mal told you a brand-new apartment was not the greatest investment? Why don't you broaden your horizons and look for apartments near Leighton that are a little older? That's where you want to live isn't it?'

Dad was right. But I was amazed at how reasonably priced such beautiful city apartments were. I knew that Mal the buyer's advocate had said I should stick to land, but I wanted to live somewhere lovely and it didn't seem as though I could afford a house in an area I wanted to live. That was all there was to it. I wasn't prepared to be flexible. I didn't like the idea of traipsing out to look at places in every other outer suburb and then buying something I didn't love, just to get into the game.

***

I thought about nothing but Spencer and buying a house for the next week. Like so many times before, I had decided after the night at the pub to erase Spencer from my mind, but his email had shattered my resolve. I absolutely was not going to reply to the email, but purging him from my inbox somehow hadn't helped me purge him from my head and heart.

Now that I'd been sucked back into the Spencer vortex, I needed time to really concentrate on getting over him once and for all. Clearly I hadn't done that properly the first time. After another house-hunting trip the next Saturday, I sat down to really think about what to do.

I thought that seeing Spencer around at the TV studio would only make it harder, so I decided that if Isobel called to ask me to go on the show any time in the next two weeks, I would say no. I realised I had 10 weeks of annual leave up my sleeve at work, and I hadn't had a break since I'd been to New York, so in the interest of a complete hiatus, I thought I'd take a break from all things news-related and take two weeks of leave from the newspaper and radio. Not doing my radio spot also meant I wouldn't have to see Angelica, even though she wasn't back from Paris yet and I had no idea when she was due home. I couldn't afford to go on a holiday, but the idea of two weeks at home was quite enticing — I was sure a little staycation was just what I needed.

I organised my leave with the newspaper chief of staff on the Monday morning and went on leave for a fortnight the next day. I wasn't a big enough name for the editor to worry about me suddenly not being there for a few weeks, and the chief of staff said one of the other radio regulars would cover my Thursday spot. In fact, apart from Janice, who would only miss having someone to boss around, and Genevieve, I could have just walked out and no-one else in the office would have noticed. And the radio station would just have to do without a couple of Maggie Rose house-hunting updates.

The first couple of days of my holidays were spent sleeping in and going for long walks. I hadn't done any exercise in weeks and it was time to start thinking about losing weight again. I was the type of person who only had to think about going on a diet and I immediately gained two kilograms. On the second day of my staycation I came home from my walk to find that the mortgage broker, George, had left me a message to tell me that Sunnyside had pre-approved a $380 000 home loan, subject to a valuation of the property I was planning to buy.

I called him back straight away to get the full information.

'Congratulations', he said, evidently pleased for me. 'I'm going to send you out some research on property prices to help you in your search for a home. The data will give you an idea of the prices that houses are going for in the suburbs you are looking at, and give you some direction.'

I was happy, but also terrified of what I was about to embark on. While I had been looking at houses since the beginning of the year, and had even unintentionally bid at an auction and put in and retracted an offer on another place, I still felt as though I were only a newborn venturing out into the big bad world of real estate. This time I officially had some money to spend. Now it was becoming a reality.

There was a question that had been harassing me for the past few days, and I figured George was one of the best people to ask. 'Is it better for me to buy at auction or through a private sale?'

'As you are a single woman with no financial backer and only the deposit you've saved, I'd advise that you're best to make an offer on a house and not go to auction unless you need to.'

'Is that because I might get overexcited and bid more than I can afford?' I asked honestly.

'Well, that is certainly something you need to be very firm about! But no—it's because your loan approval is still subject to the bank giving the go-ahead after their evaluation of the place you've bought. You see, the deposit on a property bought at auction is non-refundable. So if you can't get the loan approved and cannot buy the property, you lose your deposit. We're talking about all of your savings here. For a classic stand-alone buyer, like you, with no financial backup from a guarantor, it can just be just a little risky.

'However, when you put in an offer for a property in a private sale or before auction, you can still make it subject to you getting finance and you only have to put down a holding fee of about $1000 until you get the loan approved from your lender.'

This all sounded pretty clear, but nearly all of the properties I'd looked at had gone to auction. 'So, you're telling me I should only look at properties that are private sale, then?'

'Not necessarily. If you want to buy at auction, then buy at auction. And there are other options surrounding auctions: if you are at an auction and the house is passed in, you can always go in and negotiate with the owner; and you are perfectly entitled to make an offer on a property before it goes to auction. That happens all the time. I just think a private sale is a safer option for someone in your position.

'If you really need to buy at auction, just be aware of the risks and make sure you get a building inspection done so you can be confident of the property's value in terms of what you plan to spend on it. You have to remember your pre-approval is subject to valuation and if you don't get the money you are at risk of losing your deposit. And you don't have anyone to back you up financially if that happens.'

'Okay', I said, for once understanding what I was being told. Something else occurred to me. 'So what's the process once I find a place I want to buy?'

'Just get the contract of sale and the Section 32 from the agent—they can email them to you. Then give me a call, send me through the contract and I'll submit it to the bank to also look over.'

'What's the section 32?' I'd had one sent to me when I put in the offer on Treasury Street, but hadn't paid any attention to it.

'This is probably the most vital piece of legal documentation in a real estate transaction. It *must* be provided to you as the interested party, because it contains all the information and legal details about the property you will be buying. It should include the vendor's details, details of the property's title, land taxes, information about the essential services connected to the property, building permits, body corporate alerts and several other legal particulars.

'It's probably also time for you to start thinking about meeting a property conveyancer', George added.

I wanted to joke that, actually, I had already more than met one, and he was a jerk. But I kept that to myself.

There was so much to take in, but I was pumped. My 33rd birthday was just over five weeks away and my aim was to throw myself in the deep end and find a home before then.

***

I spent the rest of my leave busily house-hunting for apartments. Dad had given me some great advice; there were some really lovely apartments in Leighton, Monovale and Parklands. I was willing to give up the dream of an actual house if it meant I could own a decent apartment in a suburb I liked.

In my searching, I had also discovered another good suburb in the inner east by the river, called Greenwood. As its name suggested, it was a leafy suburb of tree-lined streets, and was only 10 kilometres from the city. It was on a train line and there were a couple of nice shopping strips located there. I went to two auctions in the area while I was on holidays and they were both sold for close to the advertised price. My confidence was given a much-needed boost.

It was while I was on leave that I found out the truth about Alex. I was getting ready to head out for dinner one night with Max and Jem when my mobile rang. The woman on the line had a British accent and she was asking for Alex.

'Sorry, I think you've got the wrong number', I told her.

'No, I have Alex's phone and I can see all the messages you've sent each other', she said angrily. 'I know he's with you. I need to speak to him urgently.' The woman sounded extremely distressed.

I explained that I hadn't seen Alex for a few months and that the dates on the messages should have confirmed that. 'Is everything okay? Sorry, what's your name?'

'Jane. And no, I'm not okay. I'm in labour. I'm about to have Alex's child and he hasn't called me in two weeks. He said he was going to New York for work and would be back in time for the birth, but he's not here and now I can't get in contact with him. He left one of his phones here and I turned it on to see if there was a way to contact him.' She was frantic. Understandably.

So Alex really *was* a scoundrel! I bet he had a woman in every port, as they say. I marvelled at the fact that I didn't even feel hurt, and realised I had thought little about him since not returning his messages. In fact, I was so detached from him that I didn't feel anything except deep sympathy for this poor woman at the other end of the telephone. 'Take a deep breath', I said. 'Now, have you tried calling his offices?'

'It's 7 am here in London. There's no-one at the offices.' She was crying and clearly terrified.

It was 6 pm where I was, so there was no use calling his Australian office, either; experience had taught me that the receptionist left at 5.30 pm on the dot. I felt terrible for her. 'Maybe you should call your mum or an ambulance?' I said trying to be helpful.

'I'm already at the hospital. But he told me he'd be here and he's not. He's such an arsehole. I knew he was cheating on me. I just knew it. When I looked in his phone I figured you were the *other woman*. But if he's not with you, there must be someone else as well!'

It was the most surreal conversation I'd ever had in my life. 'I'm sorry, Jane. I didn't know about you. He left me without saying a word a few months back, and I haven't seen him since. It was all very bizarre and now I know why.'

Jane suddenly let out a piercing wail and we lost the connection.

I was in shock and walked to dinner dazed and confused. Max and Jem's jaws dropped when I told them the story.

'He seemed so nice', Jem said.

'Nah, he was dodgy. I could have told you that from the beginning', Max added helpfully. He could never help being a smart alec.

There was nothing I could do to help Jane; I just wished there was a way to make Alex pay for being such a nasty piece of work.

Having conceded that an apartment was more affordable than a house at this stage, by the Friday before I went back to work I had found two apartments on which I was keen make offers. One was being offered through a private sale, or as a private treaty, as I had since found out it was also called. The other was being sold at auction on the third Saturday in November.

The apartment up for private sale was in a 1960s brick block of flats in Greenwood. The owners were asking for $395 000, and from the data George had sent me, this seemed like a reasonable price for the area. It was a two-bedroom ground-floor apartment, with hardwood floors, a north-facing living room and a practical kitchen and bathroom. There was also an undercover car space; something my dad was glad to see when he came with me to inspect it. We both thought it was in great condition considering it was 50 years old.

The second apartment was in Leighton, and I had fallen head over heels in love with it. But, unlike the house in Treasury Street, this time I could actually put in an offer to the agent knowing I could probably afford it.

The ad had called it 'Delightful Art Deco', and it was in an incredible 1920s Deco building that was shaped like a vintage radio. The second-floor apartment was in the period style, with two bedrooms, built-in robes, high ceilings, central heating and a parking space. The kitchen and bathroom would need a spruce up at some stage, but were functional. Ornate windows in the lounge room and main bedroom looked out onto a spacious solid-walled balcony, which in turn looked down on a tree-filled garden below. The trendy Leighton shopping strip was only three minutes' walk away. The vendor was asking for $385 000-plus.

My father had come along with me twice to see it and suggested that I have a builder or an architect check it out because it was so old and could have been a handsome dud. It was being offered for a great price, so I wanted to know sooner rather than later if there was something wrong with it. And George's words about my loan being subject to bank valuation were also still ringing in my head.

The Leighton apartment was to go to auction in three weeks, but I wanted to put an offer on it as soon as possible to hopefully pre-empt the auction. I called the real estate agent to see if the owners were accepting bids prior to auction, but she informed me that the owners were not interested; they wanted to sell at auction. It wasn't what I'd wanted to hear, but there was nothing I could do about it. My hopes of buying the place were dashed. I wasn't confident about going to auction, and was too fearful of the risks. I felt that I'd stuffed up so much already.

Out of interest, I asked the agent what I needed to do to arrange a building inspection. She told me to speak to a property inspecting firm who would arrange the inspection themselves. I took down the number and put it in my purse for safe keeping. Just in case.

Disappointed about the Leighton apartment but promising myself not to dwell, I decided to press ahead with the Greenwood place instead. Although it was my second choice, it was still a great apartment, and I could see myself being happy there. And at this point I just wanted to buy a place and get my weekends back, rather than spending them looking at properties!

I organised to see Eliza at lunchtime on the day I returned to work, to discuss what I needed to do about getting a conveyancer. I planned to ask the Greenwood agent to send me the contract and I didn't know the correct process for getting a conveyancer involved. She explained that not all property conveyancers were lawyers—there were also licensed conveyancers who were not lawyers, and

I could easily find one of these online. The difference was that a lawyer conveyancer would be able to do all the legal work associated with buying a property, whereas a licensed non-lawyer conveyancer would not.

'Can I do it myself?' I thought I might be able to save myself some money.

'Yes. DIY conveyancing is common. You just need to get a kit from a bookshop or a legal service. The only thing is that if something goes wrong you are going to have to use a lawyer anyway. If I were you, I'd use a professional. But that's just my opinion—plenty of people do it themselves.'

'I don't want any more drama. Do you know anyone?'

'I know Alex probably put you off lawyers for a while; present company accepted, of course', Eliza said with a smile. 'But I know a legal conveyancer called Olivia who is fantastic.'

I went back to work and called Olivia. She sounded a lot older than me and seemed to know what she was talking about. Her fee for reading the paperwork associated with properties I was interested in, and handling the negotiations of a sale, was $1000. This matched what I'd been told to expect from Jason and George, and was part of the fees associated with the loan that were listed on the qualifier George had shown me. Olivia said to send her the contracts as soon as I had them.

Feeling excited that the balls were now rolling, I rang the agent for the Greenwood apartment and said I was willing to pay $400 000 for the property. He agreed to send me the contract and the Section 32.

Two days later, on the Wednesday, Olivia and I met at her offices. Olivia was in her late 50s and explained to me that she'd been a lawyer for 25 years. With this knowledge and Eliza's recommendation, I had the utmost confidence in her expertise.

We sat down and I told her about the Greenwood apartment, then she went through the contract and the Section 32 with me. Olivia said it all looked fine, but alerted me to the fact that the property was on something called a stratum title.

'What's that?' Again I felt that there was no end to the things I still didn't know.

'There are two types of titles on apartments: strata and stratum. A strata title means you individually own the property but you are still a joint owner of the common areas of the building with the owners of the other apartments, as part of the Owner's Corporation. You have to pay a certain amount to the Owner's Corporation each year for building insurance and the upkeep of the property, among other things. When you purchase a property with a strata title, you'll be able to participate in the decision-making for the building and common grounds.

'A stratum title is also called a company title. It's one big title. It's quite common on apartments from the 1950s and 1960s. You own the apartment, but the common areas of the property are owned by a separate company, in which, as an owner of an apartment in that building, you would have shares. You don't have any say in decisions about the common areas of the property, and it can be quite difficult to get things done that you request. Banks generally don't like to lend money for properties with a stratum title.'

I was getting worried now. 'But why wouldn't the bank lend me money for that type of apartment? I don't get it.'

'Apartments on a stratum title can be difficult to sell, and the company that owns the common areas can sometimes cause difficulties. Lenders are more likely to lend money for an apartment or unit on stratum title if the purchaser already has at least 20 per cent of the sale price. And you don't. I'm not saying that you shouldn't try to get the apartment; I'm just warning you that the bank might not look favourably on the investment.'

I decided to go for it, anyway. I was putting in the offer subject to finance, and Olivia said I should be safe in that case. It was worth a shot.

That afternoon I signed the contract for the apartment and officially put in an offer of $400 000. I put a $1000 holding deposit on the apartment, which was refundable if I didn't get the loan. The agent called me at 6 pm to tell me my offer had been accepted. He said I had two calendar weeks to get the finance approved.

Although it was after business hours, I sent the contract to George so he could sort out the finances with the bank, then called him. I couldn't believe that it was all happening, and was anxious to know what the bank would say, but George told me not to hold my breath just yet.

'It usually takes three days for the bank to pick up the file', he said, 'then another few days for them to value the property, go to the mortgage insurers to get approval and then let us know what the result is. So, all up, you could be waiting for the full two weeks that the agent has allowed'.

Damn.

When I got home, I started fretting over my offer. Should I have put in a lower offer? Isn't it stupid to put in your highest offer as your first offer? Would someone make a higher offer than me? Would the bank think I'd offered to pay too much?

How would I go on like this for two weeks?

The good thing about having my loan application in limbo was that it had distracted me from thinking about Spencer too much. I'd found out at the radio station the next morning that Angelica wasn't due back from Paris until the following week, so I had a reprieve on that front. And I wasn't booked to work on *The Real Nightly News* that week, so I was still in a Spencer-free zone. The problem was that I'd replaced my worry about Spencer with worry about the home loan, and the days following the lodgement of my loan approval felt like years. When I wasn't working, I was pacing, and the rest of that week and the beginning of the next were a blur.

***

On Tuesday of the next week I received a call from Isobel requesting me for that week's edition of *The Real Nightly News*. She said she was desperate, as their booked guest had suddenly pulled out. I really didn't want to do it. I enjoyed the show, but I had enjoyed not having to see Spencer even more. I had by no means forgotten about him, but the distractions of the past couple of weeks had helped me think about him less; I feared that I'd go crashing back into the vortex if I had to be in the same room as him again. I was also embarrassed about running away that night at the pub, and annoyed at him for kissing me... but I was more annoyed at myself for caring for a man I couldn't have. It had all left me feeling very confused. I didn't know what to make of the kiss or his follow-up email.

Isobel and I had been in contact while I was on leave, and she'd told me about her first date (and subsequent dates!) with Benjamin. It had all been going well and I was really happy for her, and while I was glad we were friends, I couldn't tell her about my woes with Spencer. She and Spencer had to work together, and I didn't think it would be professional of me to tell her what had been happening. She knew we had a history, but I didn't want to involve her in the current issue about the kiss because it could have jeopardised their working relationship. I couldn't let her down, so I told her I'd be happy to do the show, not letting on how uncomfortable I really felt.

On Thursday morning I felt sick as soon as I woke up. I knew I was going to have to see both Angelica and Spencer that day, and also pretend to both of them that I was fine and act as though nothing had happened—it was the only way I knew to deal with this situation. I was secretly hoping that Angelica had stayed in Paris for longer than expected, but as I walked through the doors of the radio studios, Angelica came storming up to me as if she had been watching the door waiting for me to arrive. She was crankier than ever.

'You were busy while I was away', Angelica spat. Her pretty face was hot and flushed. Paris glow gone wild.

Spencer must have told her he'd kissed me! I couldn't believe it. I didn't know what to say to her. I stared at her dumbly as she continued.

'If you think for one second that I'm going to let you win, you've got another thing coming.'

'Win? What are you talking about?' I asked her. Where was all the so-called good value Benjamin had talked about?

'You know what I'm talking about. I'm not impressed and I'm really hurt that you would do this.'

Hurt? She looked more like she was about to hurt *me*! But why had Spencer told her about the kiss at all? His email had showed that it had meant nothing to him. I knew that the kiss was just him taking pity on pathetic little Maggie, so I was surprised that he'd even bothered to tell Angelica. Then again, he probably told her pre-emptively, just in case I turned into a crazy stalker, or in case I told her myself. Obviously he didn't think too much of me.

And it was *him* who'd kissed *me*, so why was she acting as if it was my fault? 'I'm sorry, Angelica. I didn't think—'

'No, you didn't think. It seems you never do.'

I was due on air, so I left her standing there, red-faced and seething, and made my way into the studio. I didn't see Angelica standing in her usual producer's booth while we were on air, and after my spot I ran out of the studio to avoid another confrontation.

The day could not have gotten off to a worse start, and it didn't get better when I got to *The City* office and Janice was waiting by my desk. The look on her face was very similar to what Angelica's had been. I guessed that Angelica had told her about the kiss. Before she could attack me, I launched into the details of the day's column and told her I had a lot of work to do, if she wouldn't mind letting me get to it. She looked a little stunned that I had commanded the conversation, and she couldn't seem to find any words. I knew she wanted to say something to me about Angelica and Spencer, but I was not going to engage in any kind of a personal conversation with her. Janice was like a school bully who had never had her comeuppance. I wasn't going to let her chalk up another victory that morning.

My mobile phone suddenly rang and I was able to excuse myself. She had no choice but to retreat to her office, presumably to plan her next attack.

It was George calling me (and I'd only been sweating for a week!) with what I thought was going to be an approval on my home loan. But no; the day just kept getting worse.

'I have some bad news. Sunnyside has rejected the loan because it's on a stratum title', he told me straight out.

I was really disappointed, but tried to remind myself that I'd been prepared for this. 'Is there anything we can do to change Sunnyside's mind?'

'Unfortunately, no. Stratum titles are rare nowadays, but still very unpopular with lenders. Don't be disheartened. Get back out there and keep looking. Let your lawyer know and she'll contact the agent for you.'

But I *was* disheartened. I felt as though I had no idea what I was doing, and I still felt so far away from owning my own place. It had been right in the palm of my hand, and then suddenly it was gone again.

I rang Olivia and let her know the sale wasn't going ahead and she told me she'd sort it out with the agent.

As I worked throughout the rest of the day, I thought about what I was going to say to Spencer when I saw him later that night. My plan of ignoring the kiss and just getting on with our lives was clearly not going to work since he'd brought Angelica into it.

When I arrived at the Metro studios, I marched straight into Spencer's office and slammed the door behind me. He looked up from his desk in surprise.

'What the hell did you tell Angelica about what happened between us?' I began. 'Did you tell her I'm just a desperate ex and it was a pity kiss? Why is she so angry at me? The fact is, buddy, that you kissed me and I had nothing to do with it.'

'Maggie, what are you talking about?' Spencer had stood up from his desk and was walking towards me.

I took a step forward and poked him in the chest. Hard. 'Angelica told me she knew what I'd been up to while she was away. That was an awful thing to do to me, Spencer. Now I look like the floozy who threw myself at you when really I was trying to get away!'

'Can you please calm down and let me explain? You always fly off the handle before I can get a word in edgewise.'

I was *not* going to let him explain! 'I have to go to work with her every week and you should have enough respect for me to tell her the truth about what you did.'

'Maggie, please. Let me explain. Angelica and I broke up.'

Well, this was certainly not what I had expected him to say! Angelica's advances that morning had been those of a jealous girlfriend.

'What?' I raved. 'So why did you have to bring me into it and make me her number one enemy? Or did you tell her about the kiss and *then* she broke up with you?' That would explain why she was so mad at me.

'I broke up with her when she got back from Paris', he said loudly, matching my tone. 'The night she arrived in France, she got drunk and called me, and confessed

212

that she'd cheated on me before she'd left. I just couldn't break it off with her over the phone, while she was overseas. It felt crass. Yes, I kissed you before I officially broke up with her, but in my mind we were already finished, okay? In fact, we were already finished long before she cheated. She got home on Saturday and I went around to see her to tell her it was over. But I didn't tell her I'd kissed you. I wouldn't do that to you.' His voice suddenly softened as he continued. 'She must have figured out that it was because of you.'

Because of me? Didn't he break up with her because of her cheating? Why was he saying he broke up with her because of *me*? I was so confused and embarrassed by everything that had happened. I felt pathetic. 'You shouldn't have kissed me. It wasn't fair', I said more quietly. 'I wish my editor had never recommended me for this stupid TV show. It's given me nothing but grief since I started.' I was shaking.

'Maggie, I was the one who recommended that you be invited on the show. I'm sorry. I didn't realise you hated it so much.'

'It was *you*? You should have told me that!' The shaking was getting worse.

'There was no way you would have accepted if you knew I'd put your name forward, Maggie. I recommended you because you're great at what you do—but also, I wanted to see you.' He touched my arm.

'No, don't touch me, Spencer.' I pushed him away gently. 'You're strong. You can do this but I can't. You left me and went to Japan. But I have had to watch you come back into my life and be happy with Angelica for almost an entire year. How do you think that has made me feel, having to see you both?'

'No, Maggie', Spencer said reaching out to take my hands in his. 'It's not about being strong at all. When I left, you told me you wouldn't wait for me; you're the one who broke it off. I could never have broken it off with you.'

'What?!' I pulled my hands out of his in surprise and raised my voice again. 'You made it very clear that you didn't *want* me to go with you. I had no choice but to break it off. You didn't even try to get me to go with you! You only asked me once, and then you *told* me to stay here! You made the decisions for both of us and that wasn't fair. And you *knew* the long-distance thing wouldn't have worked—you didn't want it to! I didn't see the point in prolonging the inevitable.'

'Maggie, you've got it all wrong', he spoke calmly and caught my hands again, which had been flying in all directions as I spoke. 'We both had great professional opportunities—yours was just as important as mine, and I didn't want you to give it up to come with me. *That* wouldn't have been fair. But I always wanted us to stay together. And I *did* want the long-distance thing to work. But when you broke up with me I could see you weren't going to change your mind.'

'But. No. You were able to move on. I'm still just the same Maggie Rose you left here all that time ago.'

'I might have looked like I'd moved on, but I have never gotten over you, Maggie. I've never wanted to. Angelica knew that—that's why she cheated on me. She knew my heart hadn't been in our relationship since you came back into my life. But I really didn't think you were interested in me. It's seemed as if you haven't wanted a bar of me since I got back. But I still love you, Maggie. I want to be with you.' One of his hands moved up to touch my cheek.

I didn't know what to say. Spencer had just turned the last two years of my life upside down. Had we broken up over a big misunderstanding? How could that be true? Did we really let that happen? My mind was whirring with conversations I'd had with Spencer before he'd moved to Japan. The only clear thought I could form was that I had to get into the make-up chair before the show. 'Spencer, I can't …' The words caught in my throat as I backed away from him and stumbled out of his office.

The show went by in a whirl. I have no idea how I got through it or what I said, or how I managed to catch a taxi to meet Genevieve and Eliza in town afterwards for an emergency debrief over a glass of wine.

'So you're telling me you didn't say you love him back?' Eliza asked, after I'd tried to explain what had happened.

'Well, no. I honestly didn't know what to say', I reflected. 'I've been walking around since he got back from Japan feeling in my heart that he should still be with me, but seeing with my eyes that he'd moved on — or so I thought. When Spencer left, I really thought he knew I couldn't be in a long-distance relationship because it would hurt too much; I'd miss him too much. So to me his suggestion of staying together long distance was empty. I thought he'd suggested it *knowing* that I wouldn't go for it, and giving us an excuse to break up because he really didn't want to be with me anyway. But it turns out that Spencer really thought *I* didn't love *him* anymore.'

Eliza sighed. 'Have you ever actually listened to yourself? Why do you always have to make your life more difficult than everyone else's?' Eliza looked to Genevieve for affirmation. And she got it.

'You love him. Can you please just sort it out? It's driving us all mad.'

'You're right. What am I doing?'

I left the two of them at the bar and hailed a taxi to take me to Spencer's place. I knew he was back living with his old housemate, but when I got to the house there was no-one home. I sat at the front door for 15 minutes and then called a taxi to take me home. The taxi almost immediately pulled up the driveway and, as I went to get in, Spencer got out.

'Hi', he smiled. 'I'm so glad you're—'

I cut him off. 'Spencer, I'm an idiot. I'm so, so sorry for not letting you know how I felt, both before you left for Japan and after you got back.'

'It's okay, Mag—'

'No, it's not', I was talking quickly now. 'I was angry with you for being with Angelica, but I had no right to be. I was seeing someone else for a while, too. I shouldn't be bringing that up now, though; he was a complete shocker.'

'Really, Maggie, it's—'

'Wait. I'm doing it again; not saying what I mean. What I meant to say is I haven't been honest with you or myself about how I've felt. This whole time.'

'I under—'

'No, I don't think you do understand. And I can't believe we've wasted all this time.'

'We've—'

'No, listen to me. It seems that we broke up because of a misunderstanding, which is just *crazy*. So that's why I want this to be clear. No misunderstandings. No grey area. Really, really clear. The clearest.'

I stopped. I had expected him to try to interrupt me again, but he just stood there smiling at me with his head cocked to one side. I looked in his eyes and exhaled. I suddenly felt exhausted.

'Well?' he asked, after a few seconds.

'Well what?'

He laughed. 'What do you want to be the clearest?'

'I didn't finish? Oh!' I grabbed his hand and looked up at him again. 'Here's the thing: I love you, Spencer. Wherever you are, I want to be there, too.'

He enveloped me in his arms. Then he gently kissed me before walking me inside. We both called in sick for work the next day and spent almost 48 hours locked in his room.

***

I had told my parents on Thursday afternoon about missing out on the Greenwood apartment, and my dad had encouraged me to get straight back on the house-hunting horse. So we had arranged to do so on the Saturday, and I invited Spencer.

We met Dad at the first inspection at 9 am. He looked more than happy to see Spencer and me together again. He left us to make a phone call not along after we met up with him, and I was certain he was calling to tell Mum the news.

Our itinerary for the day was to see a few auctions and inspections, including re-visiting the Leighton Deco apartment I had wanted to make an offer on two weeks earlier. When we got to the Leighton apartment, my roller-coaster of emotions continued; I was instantly relieved that I hadn't been approved to buy the Greenwood place.

There was something about the apartment in Church Street, Leighton, that screamed 'Maggie Rose'.

The windows were huge and let in light at all times of the day. Even though the apartment wasn't particularly large, I could see what needed to be done with it and could imagine how I would set up my furniture so it looked most stunning. But it was the simple stained-glass door that really won me over. I hadn't paid much attention to it the first two times I'd seen the apartment, but now I saw that it completed the apartment beautifully and made it look like a home. This apartment was for me. I knew it; Spencer knew it; Dad knew it. I had to get it. It was still going up for auction the following week, and I had to try for it, regardless.

As we were leaving, I reintroduced myself to the agent and asked her to email me the contract and the Section 32—I wanted to send them to Olivia to check over. I just hoped the apartment didn't have a stratum title.

For the rest of the day, Spencer, Dad and I watched the auctions with renewed interest. I wanted to do some research. I had an idea of how I was going to plot my victory on my auction day, but I wanted to make sure my plan didn't have any holes.

The three of us studied the moves of the bidders and decided that the way to win was to wait until the last moment to bid. That way, if I was priced out, I hadn't contributed to the price going up. I saw the same man in the trench coat that I had seen months earlier, and Dad said he must have been a buyer's advocate, buying houses on behalf of his clients. He did seem to be pretty au fait with buying houses and he again won the auction. He was the man I had to emulate the following weekend.

As we were leaving the last auction and saying goodbye to Dad, Spencer received a phone call from a friend, and stepped away to take it. I was waiting for him alone when he came back; he had a bemused look on his face.

'You know your Greenwood apartment?' he said, smiling.

'Yeah...', I replied slowly, anticipating some sort of bad news to come crashing down on me now that I'd decided to go for the Church Street place.

'Turns out Angelica had been interested in it before she went to Paris, and had made an offer. Turns out that while she was away, your offer had outbid hers.' He was openly laughing now.

'*That's* why she was so angry with me the other day?' I was gobsmacked. '*That's* why she was talking about my being "busy" while she'd been away? It wasn't about *you* after all?'

'I'm guessing "yes", "yes" and "no".'

'But the bank rejected it and I withdrew my offer. Anyway, how did she know I was the person who had put the other offer in? I must have said something on air.'

'Again, yes. She had listened back to one of the shows you were on while she was away, and heard you talking about it.'

'Wow! I can't believe she was only upset about the apartment! I didn't think she was looking at apartments.'

'She was. I went to a few with her, but not that one.'

'I just can't believe it. Did she buy it?'

'Yep, she put in another $15 000 just so she could secure it. She really hates you, Maggie.'

'I'm well aware.'

The next Tuesday Olivia sent me an email saying the Section 32 looked fine. The apartment was on a strata title and the Owner's Corporation fees were $1200 a year. I thought I could probably afford that with a bit more belt-tightening. She also said it was currently being rented out for $1800 per month, which was a good rental return if I ever considered renting it out in the future.

Before she hung up, Olivia told me to give her a call when I had bought the apartment. I loved that she was so optimistic, especially as I'd have to fight off other potential buyers at the auction on the weekend. Her enthusiasm got me really excited, though. I dug out the number of the property inspecting firm and organised for a builder to do an inspection two days later. The inspection was going to cost $360. The government's consumer website said this was the average price for an inspection on an apartment, so I told them to go ahead.

When the results of the inspection came back, they were fine—the builder told me that apart from some mould, he thought the property was fit for purchase. I finally felt invincible. Maggie Rose was actually going to bid at an auction—this time for real!

***

I had thought that waiting out the rest of the week for the Church Street auction to come around would be hell, but the week was a Spencer-filled love fest, and I was deliriously happy.

Although it felt nice having someone to hold my hand at the auction, I was glad to be buying a property all by myself—it was empowering to be spending my hard-saved cash so responsibly.

By the day of the auction I had saved $44675 and had a $40000 bank cheque in my bag for the 10 per cent deposit. I'd paid the builder on the spot and Olivia said she'd send me a bill when everything was wrapped up. I was not going to bid over $400000 because I just could not afford it. If the apartment went for more than I could afford, I told myself I would just have to live with it.

We met my parents at Church Street at 11.30 for the noon auction. I was extremely excited and very nervous. Dad had asked if I wanted him to bid on my behalf but I told him I was ready; I could do this by myself. We all walked through the apartment and I eyed up everyone else as though they were my worst enemy.

At 12 sharp the auctioneer walked to the front of the building and started talking. There were about 30 people standing outside and, as always, it was impossible to tell who was going to bid and who was just there for a gander. I did a quick scan of the crowd and was very relieved to not see the trench coat man who had won two out of the two auctions I'd seen him at.

'Ladies and gentlemen. Apartment number 12 of 24 Church Street is a rare find. It's a special building in a special suburb. Whoever buys this apartment today will have purchased a prime piece of real estate.'

He then went through the details of the Owner's Corporation and the land taxes, and asked if anyone had any questions. No-one did. 'I would like to open the bidding at $385000 for this fine two-bedroom apartment. Do I hear $385000?'

I steeled myself for someone to bid, but no offers came. The agent kept talking about how wonderful the apartment was, and I wanted to hit him. Or gag him. Again he called for a bid, saying that he would accept bids of $2000, $5000 and $10000. A young woman to my left lifted her hand and put in the first bid of $385000.

'We have $385000. Do I hear $390000?

An elderly man raised his hand.

'Thank you, sir. That's a bid of $390000, ladies and gentlemen. Do I hear $395000?'

The crowd was silent. The auctioneer looked to the woman who had bid earlier, but she shook her head.

'Going once at $390000.' He paused. 'Going twice at $390000.' Then he waited…and waited. My arm twitched, ready to jump in and bid the moment he called out 'for the third and final time'. But he didn't—he simply turned and walked inside to speak to the owners. He came back out a few minutes later and said he was going to put in a vendor's bid of $395000.

'Sir, madam—do I hear any advance on $395000?' He looked in turn at the two people who'd previously bid. They both shook their heads.

'I should inform you, ladies and gentlemen, that this property is now on the market with a vendor's bid of $395000. Will anyone raise that $5000? I will also accept a bid of $2000.' The crowd was still silent. I couldn't believe that no-one else was bidding. This property was on the market and if I wasn't careful it was going to get passed in for a price that I could certainly afford.

I felt my arm go up and my mouth open but it was as if I was outside of my body.

'Three hundred and ninety-seven thousand', I yelled. My heart was pounding. Never in my life had I felt such a surge of adrenalin charge through my body.

'That's $397000. Do I hear any further bids?' He waited again.

He started talking about the property again and I wondered what he was doing. Why wasn't he calling it? Why did he have to keep stalling?

Finally: 'Okay, $397 000 going once.' I felt as though I was going to pass out.

'Three hundred and ninety-seven thouand going twice. This apartment is on the market and will sell today.' It was going to sell to me. It was going to sell to me!

He nodded at the crowd. 'Three hundred and ninety-nine thousand. Thank you, madam.' Was that me again? Had I accidently bid twice? I frantically scanned the crowd to see who had bid. It was the same woman who had dropped out before. She was bidding again! I had thought she was done and dusted. The auctioneer continued ranting and asking for more bids of $2000. I couldn't afford that. My limit was $400 000 and a bid of $2000 would put the price up to $401 000.

'I have $399 000 going twice.'

No way. I could *not* going to lose this apartment. Not by $1000, anyway. What was an extra $1000 over my budget, really? For the old Maggie it was a couple of pairs of shoes! The new Maggie knew how to budget and save and she was going to buy *this* apartment! I needed nerves of steel and I found them.

'Two thousand', I told the auctioneer.

'And we have $401 000. Madam', he said to my competitor, 'are you in or out?'

I looked over at the young woman and I could see that her phone was glued to her ear. She was frowning seriously as she talked. She must have been finding out if she could get some more money. While she stressed down the line, the auctioneer didn't let up on his quest to bump up the price.

Finally, the woman turned to the auctioneer and shook her head to say she would go no further. She was out of the race!

'Ladies and gentlemen, the property is going once at $401 000 ... Twice at $401 000 ... Third and final call at $401 000 ...'

I held my breath and Spencer squeezed my hand.

'SOLD for $401 000! Congratulations, madam.'

The crowd was clapping, and they were clapping for me! I'd done it. I'd won. It was mine!

My head was spinning and, as always happened when I got excited, my heart started thumping. When I came to my senses I realised that I needed another $100 for the deposit as my cheque was for only $40 000. I'd gone over my budget but I knew it was going to be okay. Mum, Dad and Spencer all pulled out their wallets to give me cash, but I was able to tell them thanks, but no thanks—I actually had $100 in my own purse—although Dad said it wasn't very professional to pay for a house with change, so he swapped my $10 worth of coins for a $10 note. I was then shepherded inside by the agent.

I found myself sitting at the kitchen table of my new home, with the contract of sale in front of me, while Spencer and Dad stood proudly at my side. I gave the agent the $40 100 and signed the contract. I hadn't given the settlement period any thought, but the owners were happy with 30 days, which meant I would be in the house before the end of the year.

I was so sad to have to leave my new apartment; I could have stayed there all day staring at it. But I also couldn't wait to call all my friends to invite them out to celebrate. First, though, I had to call George so he could start processing the paperwork.

'Congratulations, Maggie', George said. 'I'll let you know how it goes. As I said last time, it could take 10 or so days, but the banks have been a lot faster at getting these done lately. Fingers crossed.'

Mum, Dad, Spencer and I went and had a bottle of champagne around the corner.

'To our Maggie. We are the proudest parents in the world today', Dad toasted, as we held up our glasses.

After one glass, Mum and Dad left Spencer and me to finish the bottle of champagne, and I texted the others and told them to meet us that night at a bar in Leighton.

I gathered my friends at a Spanish bar that we had been going to for years. Max, Jem, Eliza and her husband, Tom, were there, as was Fran (alone — the guy she'd been seeing had turned out to be slightly afraid of commitment). Unfortunately, Tim couldn't make it because he was working, but Genevieve brought along her freshly arrived Scottish boyfriend, Mac, and Isobel brought Benjamin.

The 11 of us sat at a small table near the front window, cheering and chatting about what the future held. Several bottles of champagne were emptied before we knew it. I was beaming from ear to ear. I'd been proud of myself before, but never had I felt the way I felt that night. It was a brilliant night and not even Max's usual goading comments annoyed me.

'I'd like to propose a toast to Maggie', Max said. Jem and I groaned, knowing that one of Max's famous speeches was headed our way. It was almost midnight and we were all a little worse for wear. But Max was in particularly high spirits.

'I've known Maggie for more than a decade now, and if there's one thing I can say about her it's that she never does anything by the book. I've seen her finish university but choose to travel the world instead of getting a job.

I've seen her fall in love several times with the wrong man, and then nearly lose the right one. She never has any faith in herself, but all of us here tonight know what a remarkable woman she is.

'Almost four years ago I had the privilege of helping Maggie move into Eliza's house when she was broke and depressed, and didn't have clue what the future held for her. Less than a year later she had lifted herself out of debt and saved an incredible amount of money. Now she's gone and done it again. We have all watched as she's struggled to get her head around the property game and now she's achieved her goal of owning a home.

'We think you're great, Maggie, and here's to you finding your dream home. This time with the money to buy it.'

It didn't matter whether he was speaking at his wedding about how much he loved Jem, or whether he was standing in a bar lovingly telling the world about my trials and tribulations (and achievements!) — Max's speeches always made me cry, and that time was no different. I had tears pouring down my face and I knew it was time to go home.

Taking a detour to the bathroom before Spencer and I left the bar, I noticed a familiar figure sprawled on a couch in the corner. Alex. He was attached at the mouth to the tiny brunette sitting on his knee, and he hadn't seen me walk straight past him. I stood at the mirror in the bathroom, thinking about what to say to that scumbag. I couldn't believe he was here in Australia kissing another girl, when some poor woman had just given birth to his child in London.

I walked out of the bathroom and straight up to him and the girl; fortunately they were taking a breather from pashing. 'Darling, Alex', I said sweetly. 'What a surprise to see you here! Is this your sister? I'm so excited about our date tomorrow night.'

'Maggie! Wh–what are you talking about?' Alex said. He was clearly shocked to see me, but perhaps even more shocked to hear about our date!

'I'm not his sister — I'm his girlfriend', the brunette butted in, while looking at Alex suspiciously. She turned to me. 'Who are you?' I could tell she was not someone new in his life. The look on her face made me suspect that Alex had done something like this to her before.

'I'm Maggie, Alex's girlfriend. Who are you?' I felt bad for the girl, but Alex had been such a prick that I thought he deserved to squirm. And he *was* squirming. He started making excuses to his date, telling her I was just a friend, but I kept talking.

'Alex told me he's been overseas for the past month and we were supposed to meet up tomorrow night for a dinner date.'

'Alex has not been overseas in the past month', the brunette said, sounding pretty annoyed. She turned to Alex. 'What is this woman talking about? This isn't another one of those floozies who's always calling and texting you is it?'

'What do you think you're doing?' Alex fumed at me. He stood up and grabbed my arm, trying to get me alone and away from the brunette. He didn't even seem to notice that the brunette had literally fallen off his lap in the process. Or that his mobile phone had fallen out of his pocket onto the couch. But I stood my ground. The brunette was going to hear what I had to say.

'Get off me, you scumbag', I said. 'I got a phone call from a woman in labour—that's right; in *labour* with a *baby*. She was looking for you, and here you are a few weeks later feeling up some poor girl. Does the name Jane ring any bells? She's had your baby. Congratulations', I added sarcastically.

'You're kidding me!' the brunette said before standing and punching Alex in the eye.

In the commotion, I grabbed Alex's mobile phone before making a dash for it and joining Spencer at the door—he had seen the whole performance. The next day every woman in his contacts list (the one on that phone, anyway!) would get a call from me.

Six tense days later, George called me to say my loan was approved. It was my 33rd birthday and it was the only present I wanted and the best one I could have received. He said I had to come into his office to sign some forms and that the bank would send me out all the information about my loan and the home loan account.

Olivia arranged settlement for 9 am on the 27th of December, and confirmed that the bank would have the money ready to go on that day. She had advised that I do a final inspection, known as a walk-through, saying that this was essential to make sure the apartment was in the same condition as it was on the day of the auction. Olivia said she could tell horror stories of clients who had not done a final walk-through, and who had entered their newly purchased property after settlement only to find that the toilets were blocked, or dishwashers and curtains that had been included in the contract of sale had been removed! The final inspection usually happens any time within the five days before the settlement day. As my settlement date fell immediately after Christmas, and was preceded by a couple of public holidays, my final walk-through was scheduled to happen on the morning of settlement.

***

At 8 am on 27 December, I met the real estate agent at the apartment and did the final walk-through. Everything was just as it was the day I bought it, right down to the retro light fittings. I could be confident that I was getting what I was about to pay for.

On the five-minute walk from the apartment to Olivia's office, I felt as though my feet barely touched the ground. Filled with excitement, I signed the relevant forms and handed over the relevant cheques—she would handle everything else. When Olivia gave me the keys I had to clench them in my fist to make sure they were real; that I hadn't imagined this whole thing; that the apartment really was mine.

I walked straight back to my new home, and when I opened the door for the second time that day it felt different. This time it truly was mine. I lay on the floor in ecstasy, looking up at the ceiling. Even from the floor, even empty and smelling like other people, the place was perfect. I got up, took off my shoes and walked around my new home for an hour before locking up and going back to my old rented place to get ready for dinner with Spencer.

I'd spent $430 360 on the apartment and it was worth every cent. I'd kept saving throughout the entire process and I still had a buffer of just over $1300, with another four weeks up my sleeve to save $1600 more if I put away $400 a week. My ultimate buffer would only be about $3000, but it was a really good effort and I couldn't have been more proud.

***

I moved into the apartment on New Year's Eve. It had only taken me half a day to pack because I barely had anything of my own in the rented flat I shared. Dad and I moved all my stuff from his garage and, with Spencer's help, we moved me into my new home all ready for another year.

During the settlement period, I had decided that I would have someone rent my second bedroom, which would help me with the mortgage repayments and take some of the pressure off. I was going to charge $207 a week, which worked out to $900 a month. It was the same amount of rent the previous owners had charged, so I knew I wasn't asking too much. And it was going to make a massive difference to my life. I had looked at my budget again and quickly realised that I was going to be permanently skint if I lived alone. I didn't have much money left over from the sale to afford all the new furniture I wanted for my apartment, so another reason I was keen to get a housemate was in the hopes that they would have a stylish supply of furniture to contribute...well, it didn't hurt to be optimistic!

I'd put a sign up for a housemate at work the week before I moved into Church Street, and one person replied: a woman called Rachel, a new reporter in *The City*'s features section, who I hadn't met before. I'd arranged for her to come and have a look at the apartment a week after I'd moved in.

By Saturday 7 January, I'd finished unpacking all my boxes and making the apartment look nice. Rachel was due any moment to inspect the spare room, so I made a cup of tea and sat out on the balcony to wait. I was so excited to start a new chapter in my life where I was the one who got to choose who I lived with. I was sick to death of having to work around landlords and messy housemates; of not being in control of my own environment. And I wanted to live with someone calm and up for a good time when it was needed. I hoped Rachel was the type of person I would want to live with and not the type of person I would want to kill within a couple of weeks.

My phone beeped to tell me I had a text message. It was Rachel, apologising profusely, and saying she wasn't coming because her application to rent another place had just been accepted. Damn. Back to the drawing board. I was not impressed.

I called Spencer to tell him about Rachel, and let him know I could meet him a bit earlier for dinner, since my date with a potential new housemate had fallen through. I felt better after speaking to him — in fact, I always did. He had a way of making me believe that everything would be fine. I settled back with my cup of tea and tried to relax about not having a housemate.

Half an hour later there was a knock on my door. As I padded down the short hallway, I recognised the tall, blurry shape on the other side of the stained glass.

'Spencer, what are you doing here?' I laughed as I opened the door. 'I said I'd meet you early for dinner, but not *this* early.'

Spencer didn't say anything; he just stood in the doorway grinning at me from ear to ear. Then he leaned in and kissed me and, as the Beach Boys song goes, it was like I'd never been kissed before. My heart was fluttering so fast that I thought my knees were going to buckle. He was the only one in the world who could make me feel that way.

He pulled away and gave me a serious look.

'I heard you're looking for a housemate', he said as his face broke into that gorgeous grin again. 'What do you think about sharing with me?'

It was my turn to grin. 'Come inside, Spencer. Do you still own that stylish couch?'

Lessons learned

- Seeing a mortgage broker is a great place to start when you think you are ready to get a mortgage.
- Get up to date with real estate legal jargon. There is a lot to learn, and the more you know, the fewer problems you are likely to encounter. Stratum title, anyone?
- DIY conveyancing is something to think about if you want to save money. But a property conveyancer or a solicitor will be a great help if you are not ready or confident enough to go it alone.

- Go to as many auctions as you can to watch how other people bid. This is essential.

- A housemate is an easy way to make some extra cash. But remember, the banks will only be looking at your finances.

- Good things come to those who search.

Maggie's top 10 property tips

Everyone who has ever bought a house will have tips to pass on to the unworldly first home buyer. I took my own road with a smidgen of help from my friends and family. Here are 10 tips for buying your first home.

✴ Look, look, look, and then look again. Research is the key to finding the right property. A good real estate website is no substitute for regularly attending inspections and auctions. Seeing a house for yourself is the best way to find out if it's the right one for you. It is also the only way to know if the house of your dreams you saw online actually backs onto a garbage tip.

✴ Budgeting for a property is an essential part of the house hunting process. You need to be able to budget to save the deposit and every cent put away will count. It will also prove to the banks that you are a diligent saver who is able to put away money each week. A budget will also put you in good stead for when you have bought your property, as you will have a good understanding of your spending limitations and where your money needs to go, rather than where you would like to spend it.

✳ Extras: read all about them. This ties in with having a realistic budget. As well as the cost of the property there are several compulsory government and regulatory fees that will be added on to every property purchase. Stamp duty, lenders mortgage insurance, property conveyancing fees and application fees need to be factored into your costs.

✳ Get pre-approval. Don't do what I did and rush into buying a home before you have pre-approval from a lending institution. Pre-approval means that when you bid or put in an offer on the home of your dreams you will know how much money you have to spend. Remember what Mal, the buyer's advocate, said: find the house that fits your finances, not the other way round. Visit your bank, a mortgage broker or get pre-approval from a lender online — almost every bank, mortgage broker and building society has a pre-approval function on its website. And finally, pre-approval does not guarantee the bank will lend you the money; in most cases the loan will be subject to a valuation on the property.

✳ Beware the emotional purchase. I defy you to find a first time house hunter who hasn't fallen in love with a house only to find it is too expensive or has been sold to someone else. You have to be realistic and flexible: explore suburbs around your favourite area to see what is on the market.

✱ Consider going to a buyer's advocate. You may not be able to fit this into your budget, but if you are struggling to find the perfect home or make sense of the property market, a buyer's advocate could be the answer.

✱ Use your family and friends. I received sound advice from my parents and friends and this is how most people get their heads around buying a house. You will no doubt hear some horror stories, but each friend and family member will have some advice, tips and tricks regarding the property market.

✱ Have an auction bidding strategy. Attend as many auctions as you can to find out what you think is the best bidding strategy for you. You might wait until the last moment before putting in a bid or you might prefer to have the opening bid. Ask your friends and family what they did. Bidding at auction is a highly stressful and emotional moment and many people get carried away with the process and walk away with a mortgage much higher than they anticipated. Consider getting someone to bid for you if don't think you will be able to handle the pressure. Stay cool and know your limits.

✱ Find out if you are eligible for the first home buyers grant. If you are a first home buyer you will be entitled to at least a one-off grant of $7000 if the property of construction does not cost more than $750 000. Each state and territory has different sized grants. Visit <www.firsthome.gov.au> to see what you are entitled to.

✳ Know what you want. If you are looking for a place to raise your family then a two-bedroom inner-city apartment is probably not where you should be looking. Have a checklist of must-haves, like parking spaces, number of bedrooms and bathrooms, room for a dog, or a swimming pool. But remember to be flexible in where you look. You may not be able to afford a house in your dream street but there might be a great place just around the corner, or in the next suburb!

The home buyer's budget

Before I outline the basics of budgeting it is essential to point out that saving for a house involves a lot more than just saving the deposit. There are thousands of dollars in additional costs to add to the bottom line. But once you know what you are aiming for the same savings premise applies as if you were saving for a new dress or a fabulous pair of shoes.

✶ Like I soon realised, it's not just the 10 per cent of the house price you need to save for. You need to factor in all the other government charges and levies like stamp duty tax. You can work how much money you are going to need using the various home loan calculators available online or by talking to a financial adviser. It's also a good idea to have a buffer in your savings to help with extra costs such as repairs and interest rate rises.

✶ When you have worked out how much you need to save, the next step is to start putting money away. The banks want to see a good savings track

record, so that means putting money away each
week. And unfortunately, paying off your credit
cards doesn't count! If you are only beginning your
savings journey, the easiest way to get started is to
track your spending for a month to see where your
money is going. This will allow you to work out what
expenses are essential, what you should cut back on
and what needs to go.

✳ Once you know what you have been spending your
money on, following a basic budget is your first
major step in saving for a deposit. Write a list of all
your essential weekly and monthly payments — this
will include credit card bills, utility and phone bills,
internet, public transport, car and home insurance,
rent, food and going out. Calculate your weekly
incomings and outgoings using the budget template
provided on p. 242. With your budget in hand you
should know exactly how much money you have left
over each week to put away for a home.

✳ As my financial adviser, Jason, always says, a good
way to save is to pay yourself first. The pay yourself
first principle literally means you pay yourself when
you get paid. Your basic budget will show you how
much money you can save each week. So before you
take any money out to pay your bills and expenses,
pay yourself the amount of money you have
allocated to save.

✳ Consider setting up a separate savings account
where your deposit money is stored so you don't
have instant daily access to it. There are numerous
high interest savings accounts available if you want
to make a bit of extra cash while you save. Some

charge you to take money out so they can be a good incentive to save. Otherwise a basic savings account with low fees will be perfectly sufficient.

✶ Pay down as much debt as you can. Jason once told me to get rid of all my credit card debts before I considered saving. This was sound advice but if you are in a rush to get a deposit together, still allocate a certain amount of cash to your credit card or loans. The less debt you have the better.

✶ Consider getting a credit check to see the state of your credit history. If you are concerned there might be a few skeletons lying around, a credit check will let you know the lay of the land. Go to <www.mycreditfile.com.au>.

✶ If you are paying a lot of rent, think about moving into a cheaper place or move back in with your parents for a while (if it won't kill you). It will help you save money at a faster rate, and if your parents are anything like mine it may also spur you into action!

Don't forget the many extra costs you have to consider when purchasing a house such as:

✶ stamp duty on property purchase

✶ transfer registration fee

✶ mortgage registration

✶ application fee

✶ lender's mortgage insurance

✶ solicitor costs.

Sample budget

Your income

	Weekly	Monthly	Annual
Salary			
Less tax and student loan repayment			

Your expenses

	Weekly	Monthly	Annual
Savings — pay yourself first			
Rent or mortgage			
Health insurance			
Home insurance			
Mobile phone			
Internet			
Public transport			
Groceries			
Eating out			
Alcohol			
TOTAL			
Surplus			

Maggie's favourite reads

Here are some fantastic books that helped me when I started on the roller-coaster ride of buying my own home. Whether you're looking for budgeting and saving tips to get that deposit or handy hints about the property market, you'll find it all in these great reads.

$0 to Rich by Tracey Edwards (Wrightbooks, 2008)

This is one of the best guides to sorting out your finances and working towards a goal. It includes terrific advice on investing in property, including how to apply for a loan, what research you should do and tips on saving for a deposit.

Money Makeover by Nina Dubecki and Vanessa Rowsthorn (Wrightbooks, 2010)

You don't have to have a finance degree to understand how to handle your money. Learn the secret to budgeting, saving and investing for financial success, including a step-by-step guide on how to enter the property market.

Property is a Girl's Best Friend by propertywomen.com (Wrightbooks, 2009)

Anyone can invest in property—you just need to know the ins and outs of the property market. This book shows you how to get your heel on the first rung of the property ladder with real-life case studies and techniques that you can put into practice today.

The Barefoot Investor by Scott Pape (Pluto Press, 2007)

This book is for anyone looking for a way to achieve financial freedom regardless of income. Whether you're trying to save for your first home or an overseas trip, Pape has great advice on how to increase your personal wealth and achieve your dreams.

Maggie's favourite websites

There are heaps of great websites that provide information on house-hunting, budgeting, saving, and your rights and responsibilities as a first home buyer. My favourites include some beautiful interior design websites, for when you do make your dream purchase!

State government consumer affairs

Each state and territory has their own website dedicated to the rights of consumers. The websites are an excellent resource for buying and selling homes, especially for first home buyers. Most of the websites also have checklists, real estate definitions and current property market data.

ACT: <www.ors.act.gov.au>

NSW: <www.fairtrading.nsw.gov.au>

NT: <www.consumeraffairs.nt.gov.au>

Qld: <www.fairtrading.qld.gov.au>

SA: <www.ocba.sa.gov.au>

Tas.: <www.consumer.tas.gov.au>

Vic.: <www.consumer.vic.gov.au>

WA: <www.commerce.wa.gov.au>

Federal Government's first home owner's scheme <www.firsthome.gov.au>

General information on the first home owner's scheme for each state and territory in Australia. Also has a function that directs you to your state's revenue office to check whether you are eligible for a grant and how much you can expect to receive.

Mortgage Choice <www.mortgagechoice.com.au>

This is the homepage of the broking company George works for in Melbourne. Mortgage Choice is one of the most respected mortgage broking businesses in Australia. Its website offer comprehensive advice for the first time home buyer through to the seasoned property investor. The site has tips on buying your first property, a large range of home loans to consider from a variety of lenders, checklists, calculators and information on how to contact your local broker.

Lender's Mortgage Insurance Premium Calculator <www.genworth.com.au>

Allows you to calculate how much lender's mortgage insurance you can expect to pay on your mortgage.

Stamp Duty Calculator <www.stampdutycalculator.com.au>

Allows you to calculate the stamp duty you can expect to pay on the home you want to buy.

Australian real estate <www.realestate.com.au> and <www.domain.com.au>

Both websites can help you to search for your dream home whether it's in central Queensland or inner city Melbourne.

FIDO <www.fido.gov.au>

FIDO is the Australian Securities & Investment Commission's finance and safety check website. The site is dedicated to personal finance and financial safety tips for consumers and has a budget calculator, insurance information and money tips.

Money Girl <www.moneygirl.com.au>

A sassy and smart female-orientated finance website with spot-on advice for women who value their money. As well as budgeting and savings advice, Money Girl has detailed information on investing in the property market.

Canstar Cannex <www.canstar.com.au>

A website dedicated to helping you compare and save loans including home loans, car loans, savings accounts and credit cards.

The Big Four Banks

The banks all have pages dedicated to first home buyers on their websites. You can apply for pre-approval, contact the bank and read up to date information on the banks' latest offers. All the banks' websites have calculators to help. They are currently in fierce competition to win customers so it's a good time to start loan-hunting.

The Commonwealth Bank: <www.commbank.com.au>

National Australia Bank: <www.nab.com.au>

Westpac: <www.westpac.com.au>

ANZ: <www.anz.com.au>

Absolutely Beautiful Things <www.absolutelybeautiful things.blogspot.com>

Contains some gorgeous ideas for decking out your new home (or lets you daydream about it!). Brisbane-based interior designer Anna Spiro is behind this charming blog that muses on all things stylish in interior design.

Diane Bergeron Interiors <www.dianebergeron.com>

Melbourne-based interior designer Diane Bergeron set up shop in Melbourne after moving from New York with her family. Her blog is another wonderful place to get ideas on how to decorate your home. It is simply scrumptious.

Maggie's cheap and cheerful lemon and tuna risotto

You can make this tasty risotto as cheap as you want or use your favourite gourmet ingredients. Even using a good quality, fresh parmesan cheese and a $19 bottle of white wine, this dish cost me just $7.50 per person to pull it together. Perfecto!

This recipe serves six lucky people.

Ingredients

500 g tuna in olive oil
600 g arborio rice
1.5 L chicken or vegetable stock
120 g butter (preferably unsalted)
1 handful of freshly chopped parsley
90 g parmesan cheese
1 lemon
1 small onion
2 cloves of garlic, finely chopped
1 red chilli, de-seeded and finely chopped

300 ml dry white wine
ground pepper (to taste)

Method

To begin, juice and zest the lemon. Then combine and heat the wine and stock before setting aside.

Gently heat a heavy-based saucepan and melt half the butter.

Add the onion, garlic and chilli and cook until onion is clear.

Pour the rice in and turn the heat up to medium.

Stir the rice so it is evenly coated with the butter.

Add one cup of the hot stock at a time and stir until each cup is dissolved into the rice. Taste the risotto before you add in the last cup of stock to make sure the rice is not already cooked. The stirring should take between 15 and 20 minutes.

When the rice is perfectly cooked stir in the butter, cheese, parsley, lemon zest and juice.

Drain the can of tuna and stir the fish through.

Serve.

N.B. Cooking risotto requires patience but at least you can sip on a glass of white wine while you cook.

Glossary
The jargon explained

application fees Fees charged to cover or partially cover the lender's internal costs of setting up a loan approval for a property buyer.

basic variable loan A loan at a reduced interest rate that usually has fewer features than a standard variable loan.

break costs Costs incurred when a fixed rate loan is paid off before the end of the agreed fixed rate term.

capital gain The monetary gain obtained when you sell your property for more than you paid for it.

construction loans A loan specifically for the purpose of funding the building of a new dwelling. Can also apply to major renovations of an existing property.

daily interest Interest calculated on a daily basis that varies according to the outstanding balance.

deposit   Upon signing a contract to purchase a property, the purchaser is required to pay a deposit. This is usually a payment of 10 per cent of the purchase price (varies between states/territories). The deposit is often held by the seller's real estate agent or solicitor, in their trust fund until settlement. A deposit can be in the form of a cash payment or a deposit bond.

deposit bonds   Guarantees that the purchaser of a property will pay the full deposit by a due date. Institutions providing deposit bonds act as a guarantor that payment will be made. They are often used when cash isn't readily available at short notice.

equity   The difference between the property's value and what is owed to the lender.

equity loan   A loan obtained through equity is one secured by the proportion of the value of the property you own.

First Home Owner Grant (FHOG)   A grant paid by the government to eligible first home buyers to put towards their home purchase.

guarantor   A party who agrees to be responsible for the payment of another party's debts. They are ultimately responsible for the borrower's debt.

holding deposit   A deposit based on the goodwill of the buyer to go ahead with the purchase.

income statement   A statement of income and expenditure for a period of usually a year.

joint tenants   Equal holding of property between two or more persons. If one party dies, their share passes to the survivors. This is a typical arrangement for a married couple.

lender's mortgage insurance (LMI)   A form of insurance taken out by the lender to safeguard against loss in the event of default or loss at the time of sale of the property. The borrower pays a once-only premium. The insurance covers the lender, not the borrower.

liabilities   A person's debts or obligations.

line of credit   A flexible loan arrangement with a specified limit to be used at the borrower's discretion.

low doc loan   A loan for which the lender is prepared to consider the application without the provision of any income verification documentation. The applicant will be required to complete a 'Declaration of Financial Position' (or similar).

loan to valuation ratio (LVR)   The ratio of the amount lent to the valuation of the property.

mortgage   À form of security for a loan usually taken over real estate. The lender (the mortgagee) has the right to take the real estate if the mortgagor fails to repay the loan.

mortgage brokers/loan consultants   Representatives of an organisation that offers a choice of loans from a panel of lenders. Many do not charge consumers for their service.

mortgagee   The lender of the funds and holder of the mortgage.

mortgagor   The person borrowing the money in terms of the mortgage.

non-conforming loan   Specialist lenders provide these types of loans to borrowers who fall outside the normal eligibility requirements of mainstream lenders.

offset account   An account linked to your loan in such a way that the interest earned on the account balance is applied to reduce the interest on your loan.

ombudsman   The Credit Ombudsman Service provides an avenue through which customers can make complaints about their loan consultant and have it dealt with independently.

principal   The capital sum borrowed and owing, on which interest is paid.

principal and interest loan   A loan in which both principal and interest are paid during the loan term.

redraw facility   A loan facility whereby you can make additional repayments and then access those extra funds when necessary.

refinancing   To replace or extend an existing loan with funds from another lender.

security   An asset that a borrower offers to a lender, of which the lender can take possession and sell if the loan is not repaid. Legal arrangements are put in place that register the lender's claim over the asset until the loan is repaid. Usually property is offered as security.

standard variable loan A loan product packed with comprehensive features such as an extra repayment option. The interest rate will fluctuate up and down depending on the market, and repayments on these loans can be either interest only or principal and interest. Most owner occupied loans are variable interest rate loans.

tenants in common Where more than one person owns separate, defined portions of a property. If one person dies, the relevant portion passes through the deceased estate rather than to the other property owner(s) as it does with joint tenancy. Each owner can hold a specific share of ownership and has the right to dispose of their interest.

term The length of a loan or a specific portion within the loan.

unencumbered A property free of liabilities or restrictions.

valuation A report required by the lender, detailing a professional opinion of property value.

vendor The person or company selling the property.

Source: 'Step-by-step guide to property ownership' © Mortgage Choice